THE ENGLISH VERB

An Exploration of Structure and Meaning

MICHAEL LEWIS

LTP
TEACHER
TRAINING

About this book

This book is about *exploring* the English verb, not explaining it. The difference is important. "Explaining" assumes one person knows, and the other does not. It suggests a one-way process, which starts from a place decided by the person who knows. "Exploring" suggests the possibility of going wrong, the need to re-trace our steps, a process of guessing, checking and discovering together. Some of our guesses are right, and others wrong. The emphasis is on a dynamic and co-operative process. That is, I hope, the emphasis of this book.

So often "explaining grammar" is a waste of time, which confuses rather than helps. I hope teachers will be influenced by this book to change the emphasis of work that they do with their students from explaining to exploring.

Printing conventions

In this book *have* is used to mean the word *have; (have)* is used to mean any form of that verb - i.e. *has, have, had, having.*

Occasionally, examples are discussed which are not natural or correct English. In all cases these are preceded by a *. Any example not preceded by * is well-formed, natural English.

Contents

Language Teaching Publications
35 Church Road, Hove, BN3 2BE, England

ISBN 0 906717 40 X

© LTP 1986
Reprinted 1988, 1991, 1994

NO UNAUTHORISED PHOTOCOPYING

Acknowledgements
I am grateful to R A Close, whose book *English as a Foreign Language* (now re-published as *A Teachers' Grammar*, LTP) first encouraged me to think that grammar might be simpler and more systematic than many other presentations had led me to believe.

I am particularly grateful to my colleague Jimmie Hill who has discussed most of the ideas in this book with me for more hours than either of us could recall. In particular, the perception of *(be) going to* as an aspect, basically similar to the perfect in English, was his rather than mine, and the source of many fruitful ideas for me.

A number of other grammars of English are referred to in the text, but mention of them is not intended to act as a recommendation. By far the most useful book for classroom use and for teachers seems to me to be Michael Swan's *Practical English Usage, Oxford University Press*, which discusses an enormous number of problems not referred to in this book. It is an unfailingly helpful reference.

I am grateful to Linda Griffiths for typing much of the manuscript accurately and quickly.

I am also grateful to Punch Publications for allowing me to use a number of cartoons. The captions to these say a great deal about the real nature of grammar very economically.

Michael Lewis

The Author
Michael Lewis taught English in Sweden at all levels from primary school to adult. In 1981 he co-founded LTP. He has lectured on language and methodology in most European countries, Japan, the States and Central America. He is the author of The Lexical Approach and a number of student texts and co-author of Business English (with Peter Wilberg) and Practical Techniques (with Jimmie Hill). His main current interests lie in the areas of grammar, vocabulary and the development of a lexical approach and appropriate classroom materials.

Cover designed by Anna Macleod.
Printed in England by Commercial Colour Press, London E7.

Some questions discussed in this book

Do all uses of the present simple — those referring to Now *(I swear it wasn't me)* and always *(Wood floats on water)* — have something important in common? — Yes

Are *I lived there for 30 years* and *I was living there for 30 years* both possible, correct English? — Yes

Is there a future tense in English? — No

Is it possible to use *will* with reference to past time? — Yes

Is there a general, easy-to-understand difference between *shall* and *will* in modern English? — Yes

Is it possible to use the past simple with reference to the present? — Yes

Is the present perfect used for actions in the "recent" past? — No

Is the auxiliary verb (do) an irregularity in English? — No

Is *would* the conditional in English? — No

Does every passive sentence have a natural active equivalent? — No

Is the central structure and meaning of the English verb relatively simple and very regular? — Yes

All of these and many other similar questions are asked and answered in this book. So, too, are many questions about teaching the English verb.

Is grammar an important part of language teaching? — Yes

Do simplified grammar rules help? — No

Is grammar difficult? — No

Is grammar hard work or fun? — Both!

Should teachers explain more or less? — Less

1. Introduction

This is not a conventional grammar book. It is intended mostly for teachers who are teaching English as a foreign language, and also for students who have been confused by teachers, textbooks or other grammar books.

It is not a comprehensive grammar: the second part of the book discusses the basic structure of English verbs. It examines, chapter by chapter, the important basic "building bricks" of the English verb. Again, it does not cover all possible verb forms. It does, however, discuss the important underlying ideas of English verbs in detail.

The first part of the book is quite different, and different from most other grammar books. It is about attitudes to grammar — what grammar is, what it can and cannot explain, and how it can be of use in language teaching. For many readers not only will the format of the book be unusual, but also many of the ideas which are discussed. The reader is asked to approach the book with an open mind. Some of the ideas may seem new, strange, and unhelpful. It is important that the reader understands a complete idea before rejecting it as wrong, useless for the classroom, or before raising questions about examples which seem superficially not to fit. The basic structure of the English verb is not particularly complicated. Nor is it full of exceptions. If approached in the right way, there is only a small number of ideas which need to be understood. These are, however, ideas which many readers will not have met before. They are "difficult" only in the sense that they may be unfamiliar to the reader.

What is "a grammar of English"?

The term "a grammar" is used in several different ways. The differences are important. To a linguist (in this book this word is used to mean 'a student of language, a language scientist' not 'a person who speaks several languages') it means a *description* of a language.

The linguist who wishes to produce "a grammar of English", would gather together an enormous number of examples of English, and then arrange these in some way to show how the language is used. Nowadays, linguists would gather examples of both spoken and written English. Some readers will be familiar with the recent (1985) publication *A Comprehensive Grammar of the English Language*. This is a descriptive grammar. It draws on an enormous range of examples, sorts and classifies them, and then describes them.

In making such a grammar, linguists are never concerned to reject examples of the language as it is really used. They are not trying to tell us how the language should be used, but to describe how it *is* used. Such a grammar is descriptive, not prescriptive. A grammar of this kind will be "good", if the examples are chosen from a very wide range of sources, and if they are clearly and correctly sorted and described. This work is a long way from the language classroom. The descriptive grammarian would include examples such as *It weren't him what did it.* If the example exists, it is included, and described. An example such as that just given, would probably be described as non-standard, uneducated, but the simple distinction between right and wrong is not helpful for the descriptive grammarian.

Any good descriptive grammar will be very large. Often the descriptions will be complicated and technical. They will not be of much use to the average student of English as a foreign language. They are, however, often the basis for the second kind of grammar — a pedagogic, or teaching, grammar. This is the kind of book with which foreign language students are very familiar. For most students 'a grammar' means a reference book which can be used when they are in doubt about English usage. The book will tell them whether a particular form is possible or not. It will also frequently include explanations of why forms are, or are not, possible. There are many differences between the two kinds of grammar — a pedagogic grammar will usually be much smaller, and easier to use. Many *possible* English sentences will be excluded. The book will, to some extent, artificially simplify the language. There are, however, two more important differences. Firstly, the purpose of the descriptions in the linguist's grammar will, as far as possible, be accuracy. A description can be long, technical, and complicated. Such grammars can be, and usually are, as difficult to use as a technical book on any other subject. The purpose of the descriptions, explanations and "rules" in a pedagogic grammar, is very different. Here, a compromise is necessary between accuracy and accessibility. There is no point in giving descriptions to students which are perfectly accurate, but which they cannot understand. On the other hand, if accessibility is given too great importance, students will understand, but what they understand will not be true!

Unfortunately, teachers sometimes forget the important distinction made above. They treat the descriptions, explanations, and "rules" of a pedagogic grammar as if they were general, and completely accurate, descriptions of the language. This sometimes means they think certain sentences are not possible, when in fact they are quite natural English. More seriously, it means that they create in the students' minds a catalogue of different uses of a particular form, where each example of one use is an "exception" to the others.

A teachers' grammar of the English verb

This book is not a linguists' grammar, nor is it a students' grammar. It is like a linguists' grammar in that the emphasis is initially on collecting and classifying a wide range of natural examples. Whether the classification is useful for a student is, initially, a very secondary consideration. It is very important for the reader to understand the first question this book attempts to answer is how English verb forms work. No attention at all is paid at first to how the language should be taught to students. In the early discussion of examples the reader must not think *My students will never understand this* — that is not the first intention of the book. The first intention is to ensure that teachers understand how the main building blocks of the English verb work. Certain parts of the book (Chapter 2 and Chapter 21) consider questions of teaching methodology, and the classroom implications of the rest of the book. One of the main sources of confusion, however, for most students, is the fact that teachers have been so keen to worry about how to explain to their students, that they have not always given enough attention to understanding, at a very deep level, the really fundamental problems of English.

This book is intended to be a *teachers'* grammar of the English verb. It tries to do three things:

> to ensure teachers understand the basic structure of the English verb
> to change teachers' attitudes to (English) grammar
> to change teachers' attitudes to grammar teaching.

Three kinds of "grammar"

A glance at any pedagogic grammar will show that it contains information of different kinds. Unfortunately, this is often not obvious to the student, or even the teacher. We may list three different kinds of information as follows:

1. Facts

The simplest kind of information contained in the grammar is straightforward factual information. A typical example from Thomson and Martinet, *A Practical English Grammar* is the following:

> Twelve nouns ending in-**f** or -**fe,** drop the -**f** or -**fe** and
> add -**ves.**
> These nouns are *wife, life, knife, wolf, self, calf, shelf,*
> *leaf, loaf, thief, sheaf, half.*

There are three points to note — this is a matter of *fact* ; it is *non-generative* ; and it attempts to be *comprehensive.*

By *fact,* we mean that the information given is generally accepted by all native speakers of English (some people may want to qualify that into *almost all native speakers...,* or qualify it with, for example, *speakers of British English.)* Anyone who wishes to avoid a red mark on an essay needs to write *wives,* not **wifes.* (It is a convention throughout this book that if an expression is preceded by * it is not a well-formed English expression.)

The information is *non-generative* in the sense that if you know *wife/ wives,* it does not help you in any way to know if other words will follow the same pattern or not: *safe/safes, self/selves.* However important, or unimportant, a particular piece of information may be in a particular context, each bit needs to be learnt separately. From the point of view of the historical development of English, some factual information of this kind can be explained. From the point of view of the contemporary language student, however, this kind of information is to be learnt, but there is nothing to understand.

Many grammar books dealing with points of this kind aim at being *comprehensive.* In the example above the authors positively state *Twelve nouns.....* It is immediately obvious that some of the words are considerably more important to the foreign language learner than others; most students will need -*selves,* but few will need *wolves* or *sheaves.* The writer of such a grammar faces a difficulty — why should some examples be included, and others excluded? Usually, therefore, most writers try to be comprehensive. The difficulty then is that students learn a small amount of useful information hidden in a pile of comparatively useless material.

One of the best examples of this problem, which most teachers will recognise, is the lists of irregular verbs which occur in grammar books or textbooks. Only about a hundred are frequent in modern English. Altogether there are rather less than two hundred such verbs. It is easy to believe that many students are sure that there are thousands!

Teachers need to recognise that this factual information, frequently contained in a grammar book, is in one sense mis-placed there. Of course anyone who wishes to speak English accurately needs to know this information. But it is more similar to vocabulary than to the kind of "grammar" discussed below. Knowing the forms *take/took/taken* does not help the student learn other verbs. In many ways the irregular forms belong more in the dictionary, or lexicon, than in the grammar book. Grammar, from a teaching point of view, tries to help students by showing patterns, similarities and contrasts, which reduce the amount of material to be memorised. This factual kind of grammar, while important in its own way, is different in that it does not reduce the memory-load.

A similar problem arises with fixed expressions in the language, such as *How do you do*. A complete knowledge of English apart from this expression would not allow the prediction of this sentence as a greeting used by both speakers when meeting for the first time in fairly formal circumstances. Such expressions, which need to be learnt, need a home. But shall we put them in the dictionary, or in the grammar book? We often think of a dictionary as defining *words*. We need to extend this idea slightly to the idea of a lexicon, which defines words, or fixed groups of words, such as *How do you do*. Quite a number of items traditionally found in pedagogic grammars as exceptions, are fixed, non-generative expressions, whose natural home is the lexicon rather than the grammar book. *How do you do* belongs in the lexicon, but *What do you do?* which helps us to generate sentences like *What do you make?* and *How did you do it?* belong in the grammar.

2. Patterns

The second kind of grammar at which we look is generative. It helps reduce the memory load for the student. There is a pattern which can be perceived and understood:

> *You can speak French, can't you.*
> *You have been there before, haven't you.*
> *He has taken his test, hasn't he.*
> *You shouldn't have done that, should you.*
> *She was expecting Peter at the time, wasn't she.*

Students may either find the pattern for themselves by considering a sufficiently large range of examples, or they may be given the pattern in a formulation such as:

> Positive sentence — negative tag; negative sentence — positive tag.
> Use the same auxiliary in the tag.
> Use the appropriate pronoun.

(In fact, the rule stated here is unclear, incomplete, and inadequate in a number of ways. A better description of tags is given in Chapter 19). The point here is only that it is possible for students to discover, or be presented with, a pattern which is generative.

Anyone who learns a language beyond the stage of memorising a few words and phrases, will need either an implicit or explicit perception of patterns. There have been many methodological arguments about how such patterns are best taught. For our purposes at the moment, however, the important point is that this kind of grammar is, in one sense, more important than the factual information discussed above. With patterns, there is something to understand, as well as something to learn. This kind of grammar can also be *mis*understood.

Unfortunately, language does not divide neatly into generative and non-generative items. The possibility exists of lexical items which appear to conflict with a generative pattern, and of what we may call 'linguistic fossils'. The Lord's Prayer provides an example of the latter: *Our Father, which art in heaven, hallowed be thy name...*

There does not seem much point in including *art* and *thy* in modern paradigms. Any student who comes across the Lord's Prayer, however, will come across both of these otherwise obsolete forms, and, more surprisingly still, the use of the pronoun *which* to relate to a person, *Father.*

The normal rule, from a generative point of view, is "*who* with persons, *which* with other nouns." This is complete and comprehensive for generative purposes. The "exception" is a linguistic fossil. Sometimes, such items worry teachers. The simplest solution is to regard such items as belonging to the lexicon rather than the grammar book.

3. Primary semantic distinctions

Languages make certain basic distinctions, which recur again and again with different words, structures, etc. The distinctions are often dichotomies — they divide an area of meaning into *two* parts. We have just met, for example, the difference between personal and impersonal. This distinction is important in English, in examples such as *who/which, (s)he/it, somebody/ something* etc, but notice, for example, in English it is not important in the plural, where *they* is either personal or impersonal.

These great divisions are essentially semantic; they are concerned with *meaning.* Contrary to what we sometimes think, these divisions are not the same from language to language, nor are they always as easy to define in a few words as the personal/impersonal distinction. All the same, because they are deeply associated with meaning, students will have to 'learn' them. In this case, however, 'learn' will not mean 'memorise'; the whole emphasis will now be on *understanding,* either implicitly or explicitly.

Some people believe that understanding these areas is a question of exposure to the language, and of the student slowly building up an implicit understanding of the distinctions. Other people, and perhaps most language teachers, believe that understanding can be helped by explicit statements about the distinctions. Everyone is agreed, however, that such problems as the distinction between countable and uncountable nouns, progressive and non-progressive verb forms, the meaning and use of perfect verb forms, are not things which students can be 'told' in the way they were given information about *wife/wives.*

All contemporary language teaching methodology is cyclical rather than linear. Everyone understands that there is no sense in saying *They've done the present perfect,* if what the teacher means is that students have met the *form* of the present perfect and are familiar with *one* of its uses. Students will have to meet a wide range of examples, contrast the structure with various other structures, listen to various explanations, etc. before they in any way understand the use of the present perfect, and its difference from, for example, the present simple, or the past simple.

Almost all of the general difficulties of this kind, which the foreign student will face, are to do with the basic structure of the verb. This book is concerned only with these basic distinctions. It is concerned to build up a picture of the meaning which can be associated with each feature of the basic structure of the English verb.

Matters of fact and of pattern are not ignored because they are un-important. Anyone who wants a comprehensive knowldege of English will need to know this information too. But many language teachers have never themselves had the opportunity to consider the deep, underlying distinctions which are central to English. These distinctions, of which, perhaps surprisingly, there are not very many, are the subject of the second part of this book.

Teachers' attitudes to grammar

This book has a second important objective, which may be divided into two parts. Firstly, to lead teachers away from some of the mistaken and unhelpful attitudes which they sometimes have towards grammar. Secondly, to establish the corresponding helpful attitudes.

Many children beginning a foreign language at school find it exciting and fun. Sadly, after studying the language for a while, many find it one of the less attractive subjects of the school timetable. There is some research evidence that if the children themselves are asked which bit of the language lesson they like least, they usually reply "Grammar!". But grammar is supposed to help students!

We have already seen that some grammar is no more than factual information — in no way intimidating or difficult for students. Patterns can be fun to look for, stimulating and obviously useful. Again, there is nothing that need be intimidating or unpopular about patterns. The general divisions of the language are difficult, and some students will be confused, indeed perhaps *most* students will be confused, and will take time to build up a picture of these important points. But providing a relaxed approach is taken by the teacher, so students do not feel that they should understand immediately, there is nothing frightening about these points. As long as the teacher remembers, and makes clear to the class, that grammar *describes* the language, there is no reason for it to be unpopular at all. Why, then, is it so unpopular? The answer must be because it is badly taught so frequently. How can teachers approach it more constructively?

Firstly, teachers can separate the different kinds of grammar we have already discussed. They can make this separation in their own minds, and try to communicate it to their students by the way they present and discuss different parts of the language.

This means asking students to learn things which can simply be learnt. This sort of grammar does not need to be explained or discussed.

Most young people enjoy looking for patterns, providing they are given the possibility of discovering for themselves. Some discovery methods are discussed in Chapter 21.

Most importantly, however, teachers must have in their minds clearly that certain problems are more general, and recur more frequently, than others. These problems are both more important and more difficult. It will take a long time for students to have a clear understanding of them and, it is even possible for students to learn to speak and use English well, without being able to give an *explicit* description of the problem. Few native speakers could make any attempt at all at explaining the difference between the past simple and the present perfect. Teachers must, therefore, avoid expecting students to "understand" these large problems too quickly. Too often, teachers over-simplify these problems which creates additional problems later.

Most student grammars, and textbook syllabuses, are based on a catalogue approach to grammar. Different points are covered one by one in separate paragraphs or units. Each paragraph is independent of the others. There are two difficulties which result from this. Firstly, students are given the impression that they are attempting an impossible task; as soon as they have finished one paragraph, or one use of a verb form, they are presented with another, and another, and another. . . . Rarely, if ever, do they see the parts they are learning as coming together to form a coherent whole. Not surprisingly, such a catalogue approach, giving an impression of impossibility, de-motivates students. The second problem is that each paragraph is, in a way, an exception to the previous paragraph. Students may, for example, learn that the present continuous is used for an action going on at the moment of speaking (this is a dangerous half-truth, see Chapter 12), and then they learn that the present continuous can also be used for the future. Nobody takes time to explain that there is a reason for this, and that indeed the two uses are fundamentally the same (see Chapters 12 and 17). This "catalogue and exceptions" approach must depress students. Instead of encouraging a feeling of progress as they learn more language, it gives them a feeling that the task is becoming more and more impossible.

Too often this attitude is reinforced by teachers who make remarks such as *Oh, English is a very illogical language, English is full of irregularities.* The student is left with the impression that he is trying to understand a jigsaw puzzle where some of the pieces change shape, some pieces are missing, some pieces are broken, and, when you have got the whole picture, it is difficult to see what it is!

This book argues that teachers must make a clear distinction, first of all in their own minds, between language where the emphasis is on the *learning,* and language where the emphasis is on *understanding* deep, and perhaps new, semantic ideas. They should then set out to encourage in their students the idea that the big, underlying, problems of English are understandable, discoverable, *not* impossible to understand, and, above all, not intimidating, but fun to explore. Instead of emphasising a catalogue of different uses, from time to time teachers will need to look for *similarity* in things which are apparently different, such as the uses of the present continuous mentioned above.

This book will have succeeded if it gives teachers themselves a clearer insight into the most important building bricks which make up the basic structure of the English verb, and, equally importantly, if it encourages them to believe that they must change their approach to grammar in the classroom. Instead of being the least popular, rather frightening part of the language lesson, grammar can become intellectually stimulating, educationally valuable, and enjoyable.

Before establishing a new basis for the approach to grammar, however, it is necessary to look at some of the myths and misunderstandings which cause confusion at the moment.

2. Grammar in the classroom

It is important to remember that language teaching is a means to an end. The main objective is to change the students' behaviour, not the teachers'; language learning is more important than language teaching.

There have always been arguments about the best way to teach languages. At one time explanation followed by example and practice was considered the "obvious" way to do things; at another time students were presented with examples and simply expected to follow the model, without explanation. Much modern thinking suggests that breaking the language down into small, separate pieces may not be the best way. Whatever method is adopted, however, students inevitably ask their teacher *Is . . . also possible?, Why can/can't I say. . . ?* Teachers cannot avoid the fact that exploring and understanding patterns and important semantic distinctions is part of language learning. Often, however, the way they answer these questions is counter-productive. It is easy to confuse, instead of helping the student. Efficient language learning must reflect the nature of language, and the nature of learning.

Language is many things — a habit, a skill, a system, a means of communication, but above all it is a dynamic integrated whole. If teaching chops the language up into small pieces, what is being taught is no longer really language.

Learning is a natural process, and not a process which can be shortcut or hurried very much. In many ways, students show that they understand these two ideas. The early stages of learning, where they are encouraged to listen, where much of the work is oral, and where the approach to language and to learning are both natural, are usually popular. Students are usually much less positive towards classroom activities which dissect the language, produce artificial "rules", or hurry the learning process too much.

In many ways language teachers are the worst possible people to teach languages. They are unusual, because they succeeded in learning languages themselves! It is important to remember that for every student who has learnt a language well enough to become a teacher of that language, hundreds of students have "failed". Not only have they failed to learn the language, but often the experience has been negative and anti-educational. Language teachers sometimes say *This is all right — I understood/enjoyed it.* This does not mean that many more students failed to understand it. Too much explanation given too quickly can confuse instead of helping. The result may even be worse than that — it may make students feel they can *never* understand.

An example from a quite different field may help the reader to understand. How do you react to this?:

$$\tfrac{3}{4} \div \tfrac{1}{8}$$

For many people their immediate reaction is *I can't do maths,* or *I hated fractions; I never understood them.* In many British schools, students were taught the "rule".

To divide fractions, invert and multiply.

If we apply that to the example above we get:

$$\tfrac{3}{4} \times 8 = 6$$

which is the correct answer. The strange, and unfortunate thing is that many students could apply this rule to a set of examples, get the right answers, but still not understand fractions. What was the point of the rule? Has it helped students to do the exercise? — probably. Does it help them to understand the underlying problem? — certainly not. If the teacher saved time at all, it was only at the expense of the students' understanding. It made students feel maths was "impossible", not something for them, and even something unreal.

Look now at the following problem:

A cake is cut into eight equal pieces. Somebody has eaten a quarter of the cake. How many pieces are left?

Most students find this question so easy they can do it in their heads. A few find a diagram helps:

The interesting thing is that the problem is exactly the same as the one which intimidates so many people when it is put in symbols, and done using a strange "rule".

The same problem may be put in three ways:

    The cake problem described above.

    In words: *How many $\tfrac{1}{8}$ ths are there in $\tfrac{3}{4}$?*

    In symbols: $\tfrac{3}{4} \div \tfrac{1}{8}$

A few people, who are "good at maths" find the last of these the easiest. For them, the answer is "obvious", and they cannot see why anybody else finds it difficult. For many people the same question in words is much easier, but easiest of all is the same problem expressed practically — the cake problem. There is a reason for this — the cake problem is a natural problem — one which we can understand on the basis of our experience. The same problem expressed in symbols seems completely artificial. What does the problem mean? Why does anybody want to know the answer to it? Turning it into symbols makes it more difficult but, for most people, the biggest problem of all is to understand the "rule". By accident, the teacher has changed the activity, and made it more difficult. Instead of trying to understand and answer the problem, students are trying to understand the rule which is supposed to help!

Many language practices are equally artificial:

"I'm going tomorrow"

→ "He said he was going the next day"

Readers will recognise the introduction to many exercises on "the rules for reported speech". It is important for teachers to recognise that such practices are as abstract and artificial as the arithmetical example given above.

Understanding the division of fractions means that, in due course, the student can do examples which are presented in words, and examples which are presented in symbols. They also see that the two examples are different versions of the same problem. The wise maths teacher spends time on examples of both kinds, on showing the similarity, on providing a "rule" at an appropriate time, but also above all showing how that rule is nothing more than a description of what students have already discovered themselves. The rule is not a shortcut; it is part, rather a small part, of the *process* of understanding. The teacher needs to see understanding as a process which relates different examples, a verbal description of what is happening, and, probably, appropriate diagrams. Different students respond differently to different parts of this process. If as many students as possible are to have the best possible chance of understanding, *all* parts of the process are important. The same is true for those areas of grammar where the student needs to understand a large, and often abstract, problem. It is not a matter of the teacher explaining, *or* the students examining examples, *or* drawing diagrams (see Chapter 21). A well-balanced classroom approach will involve *all* of these.

Readers will be familiar with puzzles such as the following:

Find the next terms in these series:

1. H, H, T, H, H, T, H, H, T, H, —, —.

2. 1, 8, 9, 16, 17, 24, 25, —.

At a glance these problems seem easy; there is an obvious pattern. If these examples appeared in a puzzle book they would be easy. But supposing you are told that example 1 shows the result of a person tossing a coin, H means that it lands heads up, T means it lands tails up. Now the problem is neither easy nor difficult — it is impossible.

Suppose you are told that example 2 is the scores called out by the referee of a billiards match — until we know which ball the player hits next, and whether he was successful or not, this is also impossible.

When we present examples to students and ask them to see a pattern, we cannot be sure that the pattern they see is the pattern that we intended. More importantly still, where do the examples which we are going to study come from? Either we choose them carefully, so that *a* pattern is clear, or we simply gather a number of examples without knowing what pattern they might reveal.

If we gathered enough examples for each of the two series given above, it would be possible to draw some conclusions — to see some patterns — about the probability of a coin landing heads or tails, or about the scoring system in billiards. From the few examples given above, however, it is possible to draw completely the wrong conclusions. The same applies to the examples presented in many textbooks or grammar books. The example of *some* and *any* is discussed fully in Chapter 4, but most teachers will at least have met, if not actually taught, the "rule":

some in positives

any in negatives and questions

Of course it is possible to choose examples to fit this rule. But equally it is possible to find examples which do not fit the rule — all of the following are good English:

I like some modern music.
I like any modern music.
I don't like some modern music.
I don't like any modern music.

If the examples are collected at random, the task of sorting them out and finding patterns may be difficult, or even impossible. If the examples are chosen so that they fit a preconceived rule, it is important that this rule reflects the essential semantics of the point in question. Positive/negative has *nothing* to do with the choice of *some* or *any*. The choice is not a matter of structure, it is a matter of meaning. (see Chapter 4)

Teachers need to face the question of what they are going to do with examples which they know to be correct English, but which do not fit the rules that they know. The answer must be, that if you know a rule and you know an example which does not fit it, you do not discard the example, you discard the rule.

Teachers often feel that "explaining grammar" is an important part of their job. Such a view must be a mistake — it is placing the emphasis on the teacher, instead of on the student. The teacher's task is not to know the answers and to tell the student how the language works. Much more useful is for teachers to find good *questions* to ask students about examples, so that students may discover for themselves. Much of the emphasis in the second part of this book is on leading the reader to a deeper understanding of certain features of the English verb.

Teachers need to remind themselves all the time that naming is not explaining. Think of this question and answer:
S Why is it "have gone" here?
T Because it's the present perfect.

If the student has still not learnt the forms of the verb, it is possible that the question meant *Why is it "have gone" and not "have went"*, it is a question about the facts of the language. It is much more likely, however, that the student means *"Why is the present perfect necessary here"*, in which case the answer was no help at all. Some sort of discussion is required; naming forms may be quick, but it does not deepen understanding. Real understanding takes time; shortcuts are, unfortunately, often counterproductive. R.A. Close has this to say (*English as a Foreign Language, George Allen & Unwin, 1977 page 22/23*):

> Over-simplified "rules" may seem to help for a time, but they can produce the following effects:
> a. Usage is often distorted to support them...
> b. Hours are wasted not only on lessons teaching half truths as if they were the whole truth, but on doing exercises which require the student to choose between two constructions both of which can be perfectly acceptable, though one of the two is falsely supposed to be "wrong". (Here he gives the *some/any* example already discussed.)
> c. Over-simplified rules will often remain firmly embedded in the learner's mind.

d. Above all, an inadequate basic rule will sooner or later have to be modified by a series of sub-rules and exceptions which may cause far more trouble in the end than a basic rule that is more accurate, though less temptingly teachable.

Close has also remarked elsewhere that although he has been in thousands of classrooms around the world, and heard thousands of explanations of grammar points, he has *never* heard one which was completely accurate! Does this mean teachers should stop explaining? Certainly not, but they should distinguish clearly between *grammatical rules* and *helpful hints.*

A helpful hint is an informal guide to the class or for an individual student to help with a particular exercise, or even a particular example. It is essential, however, that teachers make clear to their students that these hints are *not* generally applicable rules. There will usually be many exceptions to informal hints of this kind which are not exceptions to carefully stated rules, of the kind we will discuss later in this book.

We may summarise by saying that rules and explanations have a part to play in the language classroom. But it is a part which is often smaller than teachers think. Some things do not need to be explained at all — the factual information and patterns we have discussed. Some areas need to be explored again and again, through a combination of explanation, example, diagram, discussion, etc. Understanding in these areas needs to be seen as a process which extends from lesson to lesson, and even from year to year as students deepen their understanding.

Perhaps the single most important element in ensuring that time is not wasted, is for the teacher to remember that shortcuts — *It's quicker if I explain for them* — rarely help. Problems such as the difference between the progressive and simple forms of verbs in English take time to understand, and teachers must recognise this. An environment where the teachers provide good questions, an atmosphere which encourages the students to guess and explore, is more likely to lead to genuine understanding than methods which are more obviously convenient for the teacher.

3. Some myths and misunderstandings

Before we look in detail at two essential principles which underlie the main section of this book we need to examine a number of beliefs and attitudes which can easily confuse both teachers and students. None of the ideas discussed here is unusual to linguists, but some may surprise many language teachers and students. They are given here only briefly, as an introduction to the two positive principles which are discussed in Chapters 4 and 5.

1. Difference of form implies difference of meaning

Very often it is true that there is no *practical* difference in meaning between two different expressions. If two friends of yours go to a party and the next morning one of them says *You missed a super party last night,* and the second says *You missed a marvellous party last night,* they are, obviously, saying the same thing. Even so, there *is* a difference between the two sentences. Examination of sufficient examples of the use of *super* and *marvellous* would, if we wanted, allow us to identify groups of people who prefer one word to the other, or groups who use one only to the exclusion of the other etc. Distinctions of this kind are of very little importance for language teaching purposes. What is important is to recognise the principle that if we can hear or see a difference between two expressions there is *some* difference of meaning, however slight, or unimportant in context.

Thomson & Martinet, paragraph 204, say:

> *Will* must not be confused with *want/wish/would like.*
> *Will* expresses an intention + a decision to fulfil it:
> *I will buy it* = *I intend to buy it/I am going to buy it.*

This is extremely carelessly written. What does the "=" mean? Clearly it must mean that *I will buy it* is sometimes *similar* in meaning to *I'm going to buy it.*

This sign does not express the identity of the two expressions, but simply the fact that they are sometimes similar, which is a very different thing.

In the same book, the following is to be found (paragraph 202):

> *Shall,* used as above, is still found in formal English, but is no longer common in conversation. Instead we normally use *will: I will be 25 next week. We'll know the result tomorrow. Unless the taxi comes soon we'll miss the plane.*
>
> Sometimes, however, *will* might change the meaning of the sentence. If in *I shall see Tom tomorrow* we replace *shall* by *will,* we have *I will see Tom tomorrow,* which could be an expression of intention. To avoid ambiguities of this kind we use the future continuous tense, *I'll be seeing Tom tomorrow.*

The opportunities for confusion here are endless. It seems that "sometimes" there is a difference between *shall* and *will*, and sometimes there is not. This leads to the next important idea.

2. "Sometimes" rules are not rules

If language was used very inconsistently, we would not be able to understand each other. In fact, it is used with remarkable consistency, as we shall see in Chapter 4. It is possible to discuss interpretations of particular items of language in context using words like "could suggest", "might mean" etc., but these are never an *explanation* of why a particular form is used. The implications depend upon the semantics, so that a statement such as: *I would like* is usually more polite than *I want*, is not an explanation. As discussed elsewhere in this book, teachers need to make a clear distinction between grammatical rules, and classroom hints. It may be useful to remark to a student *Use "I'd like" not "I want"—it's more polite*, but this is not an *explanation*. The explanation depends upon the semantics of *would*. R.A. Close says:

> The teacher must distinguish between helpful advice and absolute statement. He would be justified in advising his pupils not to use *know, remember* etc. in the . . .*ing* form of the verb until they are more advanced. He would be wrong in making them learn a "rule" to the effect that these words are not used in the progressive form at all.

Advice and classroom hints are one thing, grammar rules are another. Rules cannot be given which include words like *sometimes, in certain circumstances, might mean* etc.

3. Stress is as important as structure

In the example given above, the following extraordinary statement occurs: Instead we normally use *will: I will be 25 next week. We'll know the result tomorrow.*

The second sentence does not contain an example of *will*, but an example of *'ll.* We have already established that difference of form implies difference of meaning. *'ll* is different from *will*, and therefore there is some difference of meaning.

In general, the short forms are not used in the written language, except in personal letters. The short forms are common in the spoken language. This sometimes leads teachers to the equation:

Short form = spoken form   long form = written form

But this is not true. In the spoken language both short, unstressed, and long, stressed forms are possible. As we would expect, the two different forms are used with slightly different meanings:

He's here. — A casual observation.
He is here. — Probably a correction.
We've been waiting 20 minutes. — A casual remark made at a bus stop.
We have·been waiting 20 minutes. — A complaint, in a queue or restaurant.

4. Native speakers do not "make mistakes"

We have already remarked that the task of the linguist is to describe the language as it is used. It is important not to discard examples of real use, nor say that the speaker "has made a mistake". Teachers are usually prepared to accept this, providing they are given the escape of saying that certain expressions are "not grammatically accurate". No such escape is possible. The idea of "not grammatically accurate" is based on a fundamental misunderstanding. It assumes that grammar is prescriptive — that it dictates how the language should behave. It is looking at the whole problem upside down. It is not the case that the rule exists first, and the language must fit it. The truth is the language exists first, and the grammar must describe it. With this in mind anything which a native speaker produces can be examined, and described. Taking the opposite attitude, restricts language unnecessarily. Can you complete the following example naturally?

Oh, look, there's somebody climbing out of the window of that building opposite — Oh. . . fallen.

Did you choose *he's* or *she's?* Both are certainly possible, and would obviously be used if the speaker could see the person clearly. But what word would be used if the speaker did not know whether the climber was a man or a woman? Observation of the language in real use suggests that most native speakers would use *they've.* Since there is clearly only one climber, here is an example of *they* used as a singular.

An extension of this idea, and a more amusing example, was provided by a native speaker teacher who was in an audience discussing this approach to grammar at a talk I was giving. At this point she interrupted to tell the audience that whenever she took a phone call when she was a schoolgirl her father asked who it was. As it was usually one of her boyfriends, she deliberatley chose to say *Oh, it was somebody who . . . and they . . . .* In other words, she used *they* for a singular, not because she did not know the sex of the person, but because she wished to conceal it!

This use of *they* is not a "mistake". On the contrary, it is a clever and subtle usage. If we are prepared to look at the language, observe it, and describe it, we will understand more than if we try to restrict the language through artificial rules.

5. Describing language as "right" and "wrong" is dangerous

Here, of course, we are not talking about language teaching. It is often clear to the language teacher that a student has made a mistake, that the sentence the student has produced is "wrong". As we have just seen, however, when we describe the language of native speakers we need a more complex system of description. There are many possible distinctions, including written/spoken, formal/informal, educated/uneducated, regional, etc.

Language teaching mostly concerns itself with "standard English" but it is important to recognise that this is an abstract, non-existent language. The secret to understanding the language as it is used, is to look at real examples objectively. The most helpful attitude to an example which seems strange, is curiosity, not condemnation.

It is perhaps worth noting in passing that such an excellent modern reference book as *Practical English Usage* (Michael Swan, Oxford University Press, 1980) contains language and descriptions which would have been unthinkable in earlier books. His guidance is helpful and clear, but avoids the dogmatic idea of right/wrong which used to be so common. Here are two examples of his descriptions:

> *Let's not get angry. Don't let's get angry.*
> Note the two negative forms in the examples above (*Let's not ...* and *Don't let's*. The first is considered more "correct", and is more common than the other in written English.

> *Ain't* is not used in standard ("correct") English, but it is a very common word in dialects and "uneducated" forms of British and American English.

Perhaps language teachers need to exclude certain examples from the classroom. It is certainly a mistake to exclude them while trying to describe and understand how language is used.

6. Some language cannot be "explained"

We have already discussed this idea in the introductory chapter. It is a matter of fact that the past form of *go* is *went*, that the plural of *child* is *children*. Sometimes these facts can be explained by looking at the historical development of the language, but such information has nothing to do with language learning. It is important for teachers to remember that information is information — it should be given briefly and concisely without unnecessary explanation.

7. Language in use can be explained

We have already discussed that a difference of form implies a difference of meaning. Sometimes, however, books give the impression that two language items are interchangeable, that the choice of one rather than the other is completely arbitrary. Allsop, *Cassell's Students' English Grammar, page 158,* says, for example:

> You will also meet a past tense form with *would*. It is mainly a written form used in stories. It means the same as *used to* and is really a way of providing variety in a narrative.

This leaves aside a fundamental problem — what is the difference of meaning between *used to* and *would*. The choice is not a completely arbitrary one. *(I used to go to school in Manchester, but *I would go to school in Manchester)*. Communicative meaning is extensively discussed in Chapter 5, but the principle is simple — if the language user had a choice of two or three similar expressions which convey the same basic meaning, (s)he chooses the one actually used because it is more appropriate, for some reason, to what (s)he wanted to say. We, as listeners and observers of the language, can, by contrasting the sentence with the alternatives which were rejected, form a clearer picture of what the speaker meant.

Sometimes people have a feeling that anything is possible. They feel that English is so flexible that it can be bent and twisted to suit the speaker's needs. Of course this is not true. It can be used for humorous effect, but even then the unusual uses can be analysed and understood. Poetry has been defined as "dislocating language into meaning". Certainly, poets sometimes put together words which do not normally belong together, or use unusual syntax. The effects of these, however, can be analysed in exactly the same way as any other language use — providing the observer looks at the question objectively, and concentrates on the meaning of the words and structures used. Here are two cartoons which appeared in the humorous magazine Punch. At first, their captions do not make sense, but a moment's reflection makes the unusual uses quite straightforward.

"Tutankhamun, I see a great past before you."   *"You will have a very interesting past."*

In the same way, the superficially unusual use of language in this joke is easy to understand:

> A young car salesman sat down in the office of the transport manager of a large firm.
> "You're very lucky young man," said the transport manager "I have refused to see six salesmen today".
> "Yes, I know," said the salesman, "I'm them".

Sometimes, perhaps surprisingly, it is unusual uses which help us to understand the semantics of a particular structure.

8. Paradigms do not need to be complete

It is still common for books to produce tables such as the following:

Past	Present	Future
had to	have to	'll have to
	must	must

	Infinitive	Present	Past	Past Participle
can	(to be able/to)	can	could	been able
		am/is/are able	was/were able	
must	(to have to)	must	had to	had to

My doctor can say *I can see you tomorrow* or *I'm able to see you tomorrow.* Both are possible, and they are different. Difference of form implies difference of meaning, and that difference can be understood. In those circumstances it is nonsense to pretend that "the infinitive of *can* is *to be able to ."*

In the same way if *(have) to* exists in different forms, but *must* only in one, there will be a reason for this, and it makes no sense to explain that there are two forms in the present (which are different), but only one form in the past. If that is true, it is because a distinction which is possible in the present is not possible in the past. We will see why this is the case with *must* and *(have) to* in Chapter 14. For the moment the important point is that it does not help understanding to twist the language so that it will fit preconceived paradigms. If the form naturally occurs, it needs to be observed and studied. If it does not naturally occur, it is not an accident — it is because that *precise* meaning does not exist, or is not possible to express in English.

We cannot ignore examples which do exist, but neither should we create examples which do not occur naturally in order to make the paradigms tidier.

9. Languages are different

Because a distinction exists in one language, it does not mean that such a distinction exists in any other language. Anyone meeting a foreign language for the first time is tempted to think that it must work, if not in exactly the same way as his or her own language, at least in a similar way. Nothing could be further from the truth. Linguists who have studied a wide range of languages, including some of what are normally called "exotic" languages, can easily give examples of languages which:
Have no prepositions
Do not have adjectives
Do not have articles
Have a distinction which is different from singular/plural
Do not have three tenses — past, present and future
Do not distinguish (in the same way as English) between nouns and verbs

It is a mistake to assume that any pattern which exists in one language is going to exist in another. On a simple level, for example, *information* is uncountable in English, but countable in most European languages. For a more general problem, most European languages have a number of words which correspond to the single English word *you.*

One of the most difficult things about looking at a language objectively, is to forget the preconceptions which come either from knowing one's own language, or from what one has already learnt about English. Many readers will, perhaps, simply not understand the remark that, from a linguistic point of view, English has no future tense. But this is true. (The idea is discussed in Chapters 6 and 8.) Later in this book I shall argue that such "obvious" ideas as the infinitive and the imperative are not useful when trying to understand the structure of the English verb.

10. The real distinctions of English are not always what we expect

Expectation plays a very large part in the way we look at problems. Unfortunately, sometimes it confuses instead of helping. When we are given advice from a lawyer, we are sometimes tempted to say *That can't be true, it is not fair,* but our idea of fairness and the law may not be the same; doctors will tell you that patients come to them complaining there is something wrong with their leg, and are very surprised to be told that there is nothing wrong with their leg, the problem is lumbago, which is a problem in the back. It does not help to say to the doctor *I don't care what you say, it's my leg that hurts!* The doctor knows that, but he also knows that, however surprised you are, the real problem is in your back.

When we see what look to be hundreds of colours all around us it is difficult to believe a physicist who tells us that all colours are a combination of only three primary colours. When we look at a colour photograph it is difficult to believe that the rich variety of colours is made by a combination of so few primary colours. Without the physicist to help us, we would almost certainly believe colour was much more complicated than it really is. We may ask ourselves the same question about the English verb. If we list a number of forms:

> *Has he been waiting long?*
> *I wouldn't have wanted to be in his shoes.*
> *Who's going to tell her?*
> *They must have had to get the bus.*
> *You're going to have to wait.*

It is easy to believe that such a variety must be very complicated. In fact, this is not true. The primary colours combine to create the rich variety of colours we are familiar with in our everyday lives. In a similar way, a small number of "primary distinctions" exist in the English verb, and these combine to create the rich variety of meanings we meet in everyday language. A parallel from another subject may make the idea clearer:

Think of the number 210. It can be "broken down" into factors:

$$210 = 2 \times 105$$

But, it can be broken into smaller factors:

$$210 = 2 \times 105 = 2 \times 3 \times 35$$

And, once more, into smaller factors:

$$210 = 2 \times 105 = 2 \times 3 \times 35 = 2 \times 3 \times 5 \times 7$$

It is now impossible to find smaller whole numbers, or a different set of whole numbers, which, when multiplied together give 210. (You may know from studying mathematics at school that these are called the *prime factors* of 210). Breaking down the factors in a different way may, at an intermediate stage, produce a slightly different result:

$$210 = 6 \times 35$$

But, once the number is broken down into its prime factors, the set of factors is unique.

We also know that we can very easily tell some things about the prime factors of *any* number — all even numbers have a prime factor of 2; any number which has prime factors of 2 and 5 will always end with a zero (because $2 \times 5 = 10$ and 10 times any number ends with a zero).

English verb forms can be "broken down" into factors in a similar way. The parallel with mathematical factors is particularly strong. The importance of mathematical factors is that they always contribute in exactly the same way — a factor of 2 always means a number is even. We shall see as we examine the English verb that we can identify the formal elements (elements of the form) which are "factors" in exactly this way — they always make exactly the same contribution to the total meaning.

I have been waiting contains two factors; one contributed by *(have)*, the other by *(be)+...ing*.

We shall see in Chapter 10 that every *(have)* factor contributes the same meaning to the total verb form and, in Chapter 12 that *(be)+...ing* always contributes in the same way — in a way which parallels mathematical "factors".

The parallel is not, however, valid in one important respect:

$$210 = 2 \times 3 \times 5 \times 7 = 3 \times 2 \times 5 \times 7 = 2 \times 7 \times 5 \times 3$$

However numerical factors are re-arranged, when those numbers are multiplied together the result is always the same. In contrast, the order of the elements in the verb is important — some orders are not possible and in some cases changing the order changes the meaning: *He has gone. Has he gone?*

So far, I have simply stated that these factors exist. It is worth thinking for a moment about whether their existence is plausible, and whether they are likely to be useful.

It is clear that most native speakers manage to learn and use the language effectively. If it was an enormously complicated selection of unrelated meanings, it is most unlikely that most people would be able to understand and use it. It seems much more likely that they do indeed learn a number of primary distinctions, and then combine these, again using a few relatively simple, but very powerful rules. Even if this is the case, there are still difficulties to face. The factors may exist, but it may need such a large number of examples of such varied kinds that we cannot actually find them. Secondly, if we do find them, the descriptions of them may be extremely long and complicated so that describing them explicitly is more or less impossible. Finally, from a language teaching point of view, if the factors exist, and can be described succinctly, the descriptions may be of no use in the classroom. In fact, perhaps surprisingly, as we shall see in the second part of this book, English verb forms can be broken down into factors — structural elements — which always contribute in the same way to the total meaning. The meaning of each of these factors can be identified, understood, and does have some classroom implications.

In talking to audiences of teachers about some of the ideas contained in the following chapters, a number of objections have been raised. Here, as a summary of the ideas discussed in this chapter, are some of them:

That can't be true because:

> It's not like that in my own language.
> It doesn't fit the "rule" I learnt earlier.
> I can't understand it immediately.
> It's too simple.
> It's too complicated.
> It's too difficult to teach.
> My students won't understand it.
> Some examples fit a simpler (more accessible) rule.
> I've never met the idea before.

Most of the teachers who raised these objections did not phrase them in this way! If they had, they would have seen immediately the objections were not well-founded. In approaching the rest of the book, may I ask readers to do so critically, even sceptically, but with the idea that the suggestions made in it *might* be true and useful, and that English might be simpler, and more logical, than they thought.

4. The Principle of General Use

We turn now to those parts of grammar which are primary distinctions. They are the basic building bricks of the language, and involve the search for the meaning which may be associated with particular forms.

I have suggested that the language is probably very largely, but not totally regular. We must remember that native speakers speaking naturally do so at speeds above a hundred words a minute. Even if we assume that they speak in little "packets", each containing several words, they are communicating some 30 or more messages per minute. It must be clear that unless there was a relatively simple system, no listener could possibly understand sufficiently rapidly to respond.

At the same time, we must understand that the language will not be completely regular. It may be difficult to believe, but language would probably be even more regular but for the interference of teachers who thought they were teaching grammar! (In case the reader thinks this unorthodox view is a little too extreme, it is worth mentioning that exactly the same point is made by Leech in *Meaning and the English Verb, Longman 1971 page 76/77).*

Imagine, for example, a grammarian sitting on a beach 200 hundred years ago surrounded by a large number of large pebbles. For some reason one of these pebbles attracts his attention and he picks it up. The tide comes in and out, moving the pebbles on the beach to and fro. The grammarian sees a convenient rock, climbs up on it and, taking the pebble so he can examine it, sits on the rock watching the tide come and go. It is hardly very surprising if, when two hundred years later, the grammarian drops the pebble he has been nursing onto the beach again it is quite different from all the other pebbles. All except this one have been worn away by the constant movement of the tide but, protected by the grammarian, one single pebble, once similar to all the others on the beach, is now clearly different. That is very often exactly what has happened in language. Some linguistic fossils remain because the language was used in circumstances in which change was seen as a bad thing and, as a result, forms were protected and preserved.

First grammarians, and perhaps worst of all teachers, have instilled certain things about particular language items into students over the years. Many people who have gone to school in Britain will remember being told "use *shall* with the first person and *will* with the second and third". The most elementary investigation of how native speakers of English actually use *will* and *shall* reveals that this "rule" has little, if anything, to do with the truth. Both *will* and *shall* are used (with slightly different meanings) in all persons (see Chapter 14). Unfortunately, when people use language, particularly when they write it, they are strongly influenced by what they were taught in school — even if what they were taught was misguided!

I remember being taught that it was "correct" to say not *It's me,* but *It is I.* This is totally at variance with what 99% of (British) native speakers say. But it retains some attraction for anyone who knows some Latin and believes in Latin as a "grandparent" of English. If you are in doubt about your own prejudices on this subject consider the following examples — which seem natural, and which unnatural?

> *Who did you give it to?*
> *Whom did you give it to?*
> *To who did you give it?*
> *To whom did you give it?*

Most native speakers, if they have answered "typically", will find that they have been inconsistent, probably accepting all except the third example.

In a similar way, it is possible that there may be some regional variations in how particular structures are used. Even so, people from different parts of Britain understand each other without apparent difficulty, so the differences must be small.

In general, despite linguistic fossils and small variations, it seems reasonable to assume that the language must be very largely regular. A good description of the language will reflect this. Bad descriptions, on the other hand, will make the language *seem* illogical. The difficulty is with bad descriptions, not with the language itself.

General rules

We may show all the uses of a particular form diagrammatically:

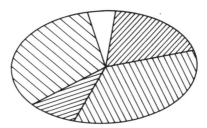

Different groups of examples are easily seen to have certain characteristics in common. Most readers will be familiar with the approach of many grammar books which list these "different uses" of the form. Some of the uses are very frequent, others comparatively rare. A lot of language teaching is based on presenting examples of one use, practising this, then introducing "another use". Each use is seen as separate, and each example of one use is an exception to the other uses. Many teachers argue that, from a practical teaching point of view, a "general rule" is the rule which covers the largest, most frequent, sub-set. In the case of *some* and *any,* for example, which is discussed in detail below, they regard the *some* in positives, *any* in negatives rule as "a general rule".

This seems a very strange definition of *general.* A general rule should apply to *all* uses, not some, or even most. It is not obvious that such general rules exist but, as we shall see in following chapters, they do; they can be described conveniently, and they have classroom implications.

The approach taken throughout this book, therefore, is different. A general rule describes the characteristics which are shared by *all* uses of the form. Once these characteristics are known, the traditional "different uses", can be seen as sub-sets of the general use, and *additional* characteristics, shared by the sub-set may be identified.

The approach has two immediate advantages. Firstly, it collects together things which have previously been seen as different. It emphasises the coherence of language, and has an important psychological effect in making the whole subject seem more logical, and more manageable. Secondly, it redresses the balance — teachers have often emphasised *difference* by, for example, contrasting two forms, or by contrasting English and the students' native language. This approach emphasises *similarity,* and, as a consequence reaches deeper into the underlying meaning of particular structures.

This principle is concerned with analysing and describing the language. The emphasis is on describing the general, and seeing more particular examples as sub-categories. At this stage, we are not concerned with language teaching. A simple parallel makes this clear. If a visitor to your home asks you *When do the buses go into town?* you may well reply *There's one in ten minutes,* or *There's one every half hour.* The first would be a sensible thing to say if you knew the question meant *Is there a bus soon?* and corresponds to the sort of hint a teacher may give a student to do a particular practice or particular example. The second answer is sensible if the question means *When do the buses usually go during the day?* and corresponds to the traditional way of teaching grammar, where a sub-group is dealt with. Neither statement, however, describes how the timetable is constructed. To understand the timetable in detail, a long string of exceptions will follow — *except Sundays, except Saturdays, except after ten o'clock at night,* etc. Understanding the timetable is more complicated than simply knowing the sub-groups. (Although I am not suggesting anybody would ever want or need to understand the "theory" behind a bus timetable!).

This Principle of General Use has another important implication. If the alternative approach is adopted, building up a catalogue of "different uses", when an example is found that does not fit the "rule" for one sub-category, all we need to do is make a new category. There is no limit to the number of categories we can make, and no reason why one category needs to be associated with another. The problem easily becomes more and more complicated.

This clearly shows when books and teachers resort to explanations such as "Verbs like. . . . do not occur in the continuous forms", or ". . . is not used in sentences like this". The warning word is *like.* These are not explanations, unless *like* is very carefully defined.

The Principle of General Use does not allow us to create new categories. An example may be an exception to a *sub*-category, but our objective is to find defining characteristics which cover *all* uses of a particular form. This sometimes throws up surprises.

Some examples

If we collect a large number of examples of *will,* it is true that most of

them refer to future time. It is not, however, true that *all* of them do:
> *Oil will not mix with water.*
> *The postman will keep leaving this gate open.*
> *It's two hours since they left so I'm sure they will be there by now.*

The conclusion we must draw is that *will* is not "the future" in English. We may represent all uses of *will* diagramatically:

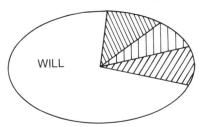

The interior of the diagram represents *all* uses of *will*. The unshaded area represents those which refer to future time. Many, even most, do refer to the future, but it is not an identifying characteristic of the form. Many similar problems occur. Here are a few more. All of them are considered in detail in Chapters 8 to 15.

1. *Arsenal play at home on Saturday.*
This is frequently called "the present simple used for the future". In fact, as we shall see in Chapters 8 and 15 it is used in this example for exactly the same reasons as in sentences such as *I play tennis regularly, I see what you mean.*

2. *I was sitting there when, all of a sudden, the door bursts open and Jo walks in.*
This use, referring to past time, is frequently called "the graphic present". It shares the same defining characteristic as all other uses of the same form. (See Chapter 8).

3. *We would go there every summer when I was a child.*
The *would* here shares characteristics with uses such as *I would think so, I would be grateful.* (See Chapter 14).

4. *Let's ask John — he's lived in Paris so he'll know.*
How is *he's lived* to be explained? It is not necessarily the *recent* past; it is not necessarily true that John still lives in Paris. Nevertheless, it may be explained in the same way as all other uses of the same form. (See Chapter 10).

In addition to these and many other specific examples, we shall see *general* areas such as reported speech and conditions, are not special cases, but part of the general patterns.

An example of the approach

Before looking at the structure of the verb, it may be helpful to consider an example of the approach we will use. To some extent different elements of the structure of the verb overlap and interlock with each other. In order to make clear some of the principles discussed above, we begin by looking at an isolated grammar problem which frequently causes confusion for students and teachers. It illustrates the importance of many of the points we have already considered.

Some and Any

We have already noted the popular explanation often given to students:

Use *some* in positive sentences.
Use *any* in negative sentences and in questions.

As soon as we accept the principle that, instead of constructing a catalogue of different uses, we will look for a description of the general use, one surprising thing appears; it is the relatively unusual example which frequently leads to a clearer picture of the defining characteristics of the use of a particular form. We may go so far as to say that examples which fit simple traditional classroom rules are, from our point of view, not interesting. Such examples of *some* and *any* as *There are some apples on the table but there aren't any oranges,* fit the simple positive/negative classroom rule, but if we are really to understand the semantics of *some* and *any,* it is this set of examples:

> I like some pop music.
> I don't like some pop music.
> I like any pop music.
> I don't like any pop music.

Which is more likely to reveal the underlying characteristics. All of the following sentences are well-formed:

> *I don't like some modern music.*
> *I don't like any modern music.*
>
> *Someone in the enquiry office will be able to help you.*
> *Anyone in the enquiry office will be able to help you.*
>
> *Is there someone here on Saturdays?*
> *Is there anyone here on Saturdays?*

These examples clearly indicate that the "rule" just quoted is nonsense. Teachers and books sometimes go to considerable lengths to "explain away" what are seen as exceptions to the rule so that we sometimes meet:
> *Would you like some more tea?*
> *Could I borrow some money?*
explained as "not really questions, but polite requests or offers". It is true that the examples do have these functions, but the student is effectively being told: Use "any" in "certain types" of question — without being told what those types are.

The "polite request" explanation concerns only contextual, communicative meaning, not the primary semantics of the *some/any* distinction.

What we need is not to explain away "exceptions", but to question the validity of the original rule. Teachers suspect this when, considering the first pair of sentences, they say *Ah yes, you can say that but with a different meaning.* That is the whole point — both sentences in each pair are well-formed, but the two sentences have different meanings. The use of *some* and *any* is not a question of form, but of meaning. The difference of meaning of each pair of sentences depends precisely on the general difference of meaning between *some* and *any.* The real explanation is not difficult. Both *some* and *any* are used with indefinite reference.

Some is used if the idea is *restricted* or *limited* in some way.

Any is used if the idea is *unrestricted* or *unlimited.*

Any applies to all or none; *some* applies to part.

The restriction may be a real one — *There's some cheese in the fridge* — or a psychological one existing only in the mind of the speaker — *Would you like something to eat?*

The real semantic distinction is as simple as that, and applies to *all* uses of *some* and *any.*

The distinction has certain implications — for example the difference between: *Can I get you something to eat?* and *Can I get you anything to eat?*

It is true that the former is more likely if the speaker anticipates the answer *Yes,* while the latter is associated with more open questions. This connotational difference, however, *arises from* the fundamental difference of meaning. As we see in Chapter 5 the communicative process involves *two* interpretive processes — one by the speaker and one by the listener. The choice of alternative grammatical items lies wholly with the speaker; the de-coding process lies wholly with the hearer. In the example, the choice of *something* or *anything* lies with the speaker and reflects that person's understanding of the situation. The listener apparently uses a process something as follows:

"He is willing and able to get me something." or "He has used an unlimited form *(any)* — why? He has given no thought to what he will give me. It is an open question. What would an open question mean in the present circumstances — time of day, arrangements we have made for eating, etc.".

This interpretive process depends upon the fact that the speaker has *already* made a choice. The choice of words provides the connotations. The semantic connotations provide the social connotations. The social connotation cannot explain the grammatical choice.

The rule stated above is abstract, but not particularly so and, unlike the general classroom hint *(some/* positive, *any/* negatives and questions), it is completely comprehensive, explaining *all* uses of *some* and *any.* The Principle of General Use is followed.

Of course it would be very confusing to present students with randomly-chosen examples of *some* and *any* when they first meet these grammatical items. It does seem, however, that the teaching procedure which involves presenting *some* in positives *(There are some pencils on the table),* and *any* in negatives *(Juan hasn't any money),* is unsatisfactory, unless at the same time teachers draw attention to the wider rule.

There is a very simple explanation available for even the youngest classes — teachers may use a gesture of their hands converging (but not meeting) to suggest "restricted", while a diverging gesture suggests "unrestricted".

Teachers may also like to introduce *some* and *any* to a class in the following concrete way. It makes clear from the start the real distinction in the meaning of the two words but is also easy for school pupils to understand.

Put these sentences on the blackboard:
1. I like some pop music.
2. I like any pop music.
3. I don't like some pop music.
4. I don't like any pop music.
Explain that this diagram represents all the pop music in the world:

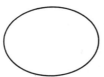

The pop music which *I like* is to be shaded. Ask students to make four drawings, one for each of the sentences. If they do it correctly this will be the result.

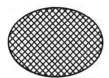

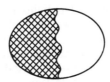

I like any pop music.   **I like some pop music.**

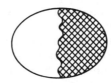

I don't like any pop music.   **I don't like some pop music.**

Everyone can see immediately that both *some* diagrams are partly shaded and partly not; with *any*, the *whole* diagram is either shaded or not. *Some* divides into parts; *any* is complete — about all or none.

(Warning – the drawing is an analogy, and not a perfect one. Sentences like *I like hardly any pop music* will of course produce a drawing which is almost completely unshaded. The reason is that the restriction lies not in *any*, but in *hardly (scarcely, almost)*. While this is not a problem in initial presentation, teachers should be aware that when students meet sentences of this type the diagram analogy breaks down.)

Some classroom implications

If the difference between, for example, the present simple and the present continuous, is to be understood, not only must "obvious" (and slightly absurd) classroom examples such as *She's reading, She reads a lot of books*, be considered but also those examples which explore the *boundary* of the semantics of the two forms. This means that instead of, as it were, sitting safely in the middle of the area covered by a particular grammatical form, we will need to consider contrasting pairs of examples such as:

Where do you live?	When do we leave?	Do you feel better now?
Where are you living?	When are we leaving?	Are you feeling better now?

It must be clear that this approach has important pedagogical implications. Traditionally, "different uses" of a form have been presented one by one. Teachers have feared students producing an example which is natural English, but not an example of the use being studied at that time. This has frequently forced teachers into the absurd statement *Yes, that's correct, but it's not what I'm looking for. You'll learn about that later.* A pedagogical approach which insists on presenting uses one by one separately cannot avoid this problem.

I should make clear that I am not suggesting that students should be presented with a large *random* collection of examples the first time they meet a new structure. This would be daunting and de-motivating. What is important, is for the *teachers* to understand the general rule. They then have a rigid framework within which the so-called "different uses" may be identified. And the fact remains that less frequent uses, and contrastive pairs, are often the best way to lead students to the defining characteristics of a form. Providing that teachers remember that language learning is a cyclical process — students will need to return again and again to the *same* grammatical problems over a period of time — and are not afraid to introduce the unusual or contrastive examples at an appropriate point — the general rule will help both teacher and student. It is not a question of *presenting* the students with the general rule, but of leading them towards it by a gradual step-by-step process.

It is worth emphasising two warnings — teachers do their students a disservice if they present the general rules, and hope students will understand and benefit from them. Equally, they do their students a disservice if they rely on the presentation of partial rules, covering a sub-set of examples, and introduce large numbers of "exceptions". The correct approach must be to present the general rule clearly, return to re-presentation of it from time to time, and on a day-to-day basis provide the kind of helpful hint which will help students with particular sub-groups while gradually trying to build a deeper understanding of the general rule.

Language learning involves more than understanding. Students also need practice in using forms accurately and spontaneously. For this reason teachers may well want to do traditional practices. There are, however, several important modifications in principle:

1. Students are made aware that there is a single rule which covers all examples.

2. The framework is provided so they can see that an example which does not follow a classroom hint, is *not* an "exception".

3. The teaching procedure must not hide examples so that a partial rule may be taught and defended.

My own strong preference, if students are to be given a rule at all, is to present students with the full rule at an early stage of the teaching *even if they do not understand it at that stage.* In this way they are reassured that a rule does exist, and each time a so-called "different use" of the point in question is met, any hints can be seen as *parts*, within the framework of the general rule. Each part helps build gradually towards students' understanding. This seems greatly preferable to the presentation of a gross over-simplification which solves problems at one stage of the teaching programme, only to create problems later.

Two problems

Before reading the next chapter, the reader is invited to consider two sets of problems. First look at these examples below, and judge whether each example is, or is not natural English.

1. a. I don't like some pop music.
   b. I don't like any pop music
   c. I like some pop music.
   d. I like any pop music.

2. a. Someone must have taken it, mustn't he.
   b. Someone must have taken it, mustn't they.

3. a. That shop has a wonderful range of cheese.
   b. That shop has a wonderful range of cheeses.

4. a. He said he didn't eat meat.
   b. He said he doesn't eat meat.

5. a. Do you remember the time we went to Canterbury?
   b. Are you remembering the time we went to Canterbury?

6. a. Are you going on Saturday?
   b. Are you going to go on Saturday?

7. a. Can you come tomorrow?
   b. Could you come tomorrow?

8. a. I cut the grass while Paul was getting the dinner.
   b. I was cutting the grass while Paul was getting the dinner.
   c. I cut the grass while Paul got the dinner.
   d. I was cutting the grass while Paul got the dinner.

9. a. We are leaving tomorrow.
   b. We leave tomorrow.
   c. We are going to leave tomorrow.
   d. We'll leave tomorrow.
   e. We'll be leaving tomorrow.
   f. We are to leave tomorrow.

10. a. We came here a lot when I was a child.
   b. We used to come here a lot when I was a child.
   c. We would come here a lot when I was a child.

In fact, all of the examples are completely natural. It is often the contrasts between pairs and groups of examples of this kind which are particularly revealing of the underlying semantics of the forms used.

The second problem is to consider the examples below. The *Comment* column asks readers *not* how they would explain these to a class, but the more fundamental question of why a particular form is used, and how it relates to other examples of that form.

All of the first examples show a form used where the time referred to is not that we expect from the traditional name of the verb form. The question for all of these examples is whether "unusual" uses are similar to, or different from the "obvious" use of the same form.

Example	**Comment**
1. I'm catching the 8.30 tomorrow.	Present for future time
2. The race starts at 3pm.	Present for future time
3. What name was it please?	Past for present time
4. In he comes and hits me.	Present for past time
5. They will be there by now.	*Will* for past time
6. I'd tell you if I knew.	Past for future time
7. It's time we left.	Past for present time
8. I wish she loved me.	Past for present or general time
9. Dinner is at six o'clock usually.	General
Dinner is earlier tomorrow.	Specific, future time
10. Water boils at 100°C.	Not present, general time reference
11. Are you going to go on Saturday?	*Going to* with **(go)**
Are you going on Saturday?	
12. I've been waiting since Christmas.	Incomplete — still waiting
It's here at last — I've been waiting	Complete — the waiting now over
for this since Christmas.	Is "completeness" important?
13. This forest hasn't changed for 2000	'Near' past time
years.	'Far' past time
I've seen Jack twice recently.	Is "nearness" important?
14. Do you feel better?	Simple and continuous both possible
Are you feeling better?	
15. Did you ever see such a mess?	Past simple, present perfect
Have you ever seen such a mess?	both possible
16. I was going to ring you yesterday.	Referring to past time
I was going to ring you tomorrow.	Referring to future time
17. He said he never ate meat.	What's the difference?
He said he never eats meat.	
18. He told me he'll be there tomorrow.	What's the difference?
He told me he'd be there tomorrow.	
19. Can you come tomorrow?	What's the difference?
Could you come tomorrow?	
20. John might/could tell us.	*might/could* referring to future time
21. Stop it! You're being silly...	*(be)* in the continuous
22. It would be lovely to see you.	Is *would* the conditional?
23. I would think we would be there by eight.	Why two *woulds* together?
24. She must have had to wait at the chemists.	Why *must* and *(have)* to together?

It must be emphasised that all the examples are natural, and that explanations based on "exceptions" are *not* necessary. In each case these examples are part of general patterns which are discussed fully in later chapters.

5. The Importance of the Speaker

We come now to probably the most important single idea which we need to establish before examining the forms of the verb in detail.

Communicative Meaning

All language is used in a particular context. We define as the *communicative meaning* the way a particular utterance will be interpreted in a particular context. Several factors will contribute to this communicative meaning:

a.   The semantics of the words and structures used.
b.   The expectations of the speaker in the situation.
c.   The expectations of the listener in the situation.
d.   The environment in which the language is used.

Language teaching has recently recognised the importance of context and expectation in talking about functions. The following dialogue is not at all surprising:

A It's warm in here.
B Would you like me to open the window?

In context, **B** has interpreted *It's warm in here* as either a complaint or a request. It is easy to think of another situation in which the same words could express relief or satisfaction.

In normal life we are exclusively concerned with communicative meaning. We have no interest in the communicative process itself, and in the difference between the fundamental semantics of words and phrases, and the contribution of expectation and environment to total meaning. If, however, we wish to study the language, and search for the underlying meaning of a particular form, we need to try to separate the contribution made to total meaning by the semantics of the form from the contributions of expectation and context. We may see communication as a sequence:

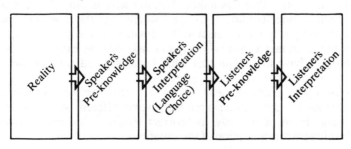

The importance of the speaker

Both the speaker and the listener contribute inter-pretations to the whole process. Very often the same basic information can be given in different words. Asked to describe this bottle I may say *It's half full,* or *It's half empty.* Both statements are true. The choice depends on how I view the situation on a particular occasion.

In a similar way the speaker has a free choice between *John is older than Peter, isn't he?* and *Peter isn't as old as John, is he?* On this occasion both sentences express the same basic information, but each provides a slightly different interpretation.

In the following, each of B's responses is correct English, but again there are two different interpretations of the the facts:

A   He's 29.
B   Really - as old/young as that!

It is not, of course, that the word *young* changes its meaning. The word has a meaning which can be looked up in the dictionary. In context, however, a more complex meaning can be created by the relationship between the basic meaning of the word, and the other factors we have discussed.

Even if we are fully aware of the external context in which language is used we cannot, without *complete* insight into the speaker's motivation, atti-tude, presuppositions etc, decide precisely the language that speaker would use in that particular context. All the grammarian can do is to collect, classify, and describe examples of language *after* they have been used, without being sure of all the details of the context in which they were used. In most cases it is still possible to find coherent and describable patterns. Occasionally an example occurs in which the only reaction a descriptive linguist can produce is to say *That is what was said, but I do not understand the reasons why the speaker said it in that way.*

So far, we have seen that the speaker exercises certain choices when speaking. These depend both on the objective facts and on the speaker's understanding and interpretation at the moment of speaking. If I see some-one getting into your car as we stand talking in a car park I may, for example,

— Believe I recognise your wife and say nothing.
— Believe I recognise your wife, for whom we are waiting, and say *Ah, there's Carol now.*
— Believe someone is stealing your car, so shout *Quick, someone's taking your car.*

There are many other possibilities but, in each case, my choice is condi-tioned by my understanding of the *total* situation at the moment I speak. I may of course partly misunderstand the situation. If the lady I thought was your wife was in fact a thief you may well ask *Why on earth didn't you say something?* I have to explain that what I said seemed appropriate to the situation as I understood it *at the time I spoke.*

All of these examples lead us to a single, simple, but extremely important idea — the speaker often has several different ways of saying the same thing. Each of the ways is "correct English", but each provides a slightly different interpretation of the situation.

In the examples we have looked at so far the speaker has either under-stood the situation from two different points of view, or wished to place a different emphasis on the fact (as with the half-full or half-empty bottle). We come now to a more surprising, and much more important idea in the study of grammar. Language is much more subtle than we sometimes realise. Its users have a wider range of choices available to them than is sometimes recognised. All of the following are natural correct English:

1 a. We met in London.
  b. We met at London.

2 a. I lived there for twelve years.
  b. I was living there for twelve years. (see Chapters 9 and 12.)

3 a. Did you see David?
  b. Have you seen David? (see Chapters 9 and 10.)

4 a. Where do you live?
  b. Where are you living?

5 a. I expect so.
  b. I would expect so. (see Chapter 14.)

All of the sentences are correct English. The two sentences of each pair "have the same meaning", if by that we mean that they give the same factual information. There is, however, some *difference* of meaning between the sentences of each pair. If a native speaker used one sentence of a pair rather than the other it is because one sentence was closer to the speaker's inter-pretation of the facts. The sentence the speaker uses is *chosen,* and not at random. It is chosen because the speaker needs the additional connotational meanings of the chosen form rather than the form which was not chosen.

This leads us to a statement which comes as a surprise to many teachers — GRAMMAR IS NOT ONLY A MATTER OF FACT.

Grammar as fact

Certain forms of the language are agreed to be standard. No one has any choice about these matters — they are grammar as fact. Here are some examples:

One boy, book, pen	Two boy*s*, book*s*, pen*s*
One knife	Two kniv*es*
I/you/we/they walk	He/she/it walk*s*
Walked, looked, painted	*Came, went, bought*

These examples are straightforward and do not require explanation or discussion — the only "explanation" which could be offered is *English is like that.*

There are many more complicated examples of grammar as fact. An example is the rules of word order. There are important differences of meaning between the pairs:

The police rang the man.	You were waiting.
The man rang the police.	Were you waiting?

Less obviously, certain intonation patterns carry particular connotational meanings, so that a word order which is associated with statements may function as a question if a particular intonation pattern is used. This is only possible if there is agreement among language users about the significance of particular patterns. They, too, belong to the factual features of the language.

Readers will not be surprised by the idea of grammar as fact. The surprising feature is that not all grammar is in this category. We may be able to look up in a reference book whether a particular sentence is or is not *possible*. We cannot, however, explain why the speaker used a particular piece of language by reference only to objective rules. Language is not only a matter of fact.

Grammar as choice

We have already seen pairs of sentences both of which follow the rules of grammar as fact - in other words they are "correct" standard English. We know, however, that *both* are correct, and refer to the same facts. Any difference of meaning between the two sentences of a pair is, therefore, not something we can decide objectively. The differences are based on a *choice* made by the speaker at the moment the language was used. The importance of this idea is impossible to over-estimate. In addition to grammar as fact, we must consider grammar as choice. The choices are made by the speaker. The speaker's understanding of the situation, intentions, and interpretation of the facts are central to the language the speaker uses.

An example

We have already mentioned this pair:
We met in London.   *We met at London.*
Some readers may be surprised by the second sentence, and even wonder if it is natural English. It is, and it provides us with an important example. Native speakers do not choose their prepositions according to rules such as *"In" with cities, "at" with small places;* they have never met such rules! They choose a preposition which most accurately conveys the meaning they intend at the moment of speaking. The most common preposition with *London* is almost certainly *in.* The reason for this is that with such places we frequently wish to talk about the idea of enclosure, "in-ness". Because we wish to talk about "in-ness", the preposition *in* is appropriate.

Some years ago I remarked to a friend *I wonder what the weather's like at Stockholm?* Can the reader work out where I was when I asked this question? I have used the example on numerous occasions in talks and workshops on grammar. Almost always someone in the audience immediately says *You were travelling - on an aeroplane perhaps.* In fact, I was at the airport, on my way to Stockholm. In those circumstances I thought of Stockholm as a point in space, and therefore subconsciously chose *at* rather than *in.*

It is of course not the case that the speaker who says *at London* does not know the size of London, or has forgotten the size of London; what matters is that, at the moment of speaking, the size of London is not important. If the speaker is interested in in-ness, (s)he chooses *in;* if (s)he is interested in at-ness, (s)he chooses *at*. Objective reality means that certain perceptions, and therefore certain forms of language, will be much more common than others. It does not mean, however, that others are not possible.

The second example above:

I lived there for twelve years.   *I was living there for twelve years.*

is similar. The phrase *for twelve years* is the same in each case, and suggests that the speaker has the same understanding of the temporal features of the situation. This is not so. Allsop, in *Cassell's Students' English Grammar, page 148*, says:

> Every verb form has two elements of meaning:
> Time — the time at which the action happens.
> Attitude — our interest in the action, the way we see it.

Objectively, the time involved in the two examples just given is identical — 12 years. What is different is what Allsop has called *attitude*, and what in this book is usually called the speaker's *interpretation*. This example is discussed in more detail in Chapters 9 and 12, but the central idea for the reader to grasp is that grammar is both a matter of fact, something objectively determined *and* a matter of the speaker's choice. Grammar as choice is not a matter of being "right" or "wrong". If we want to understand the full message the speaker gives, we need to look objectively at the language the speaker uses, and compare it with other possible choices which express the same objective (referential) meaning. By understanding the connotational meaning of those forms which the speaker has not chosen, we may more clearly see the connotations of the form which has been chosen. In this way we may understand more of the speaker's full message.

The concept of grammar as choice raises some difficulties. Not all native speakers have the same command of their language. Although we do not meet native speakers of English who appear not to know the continuous forms, we can never know whether different native speakers have different degrees of insight into the meaning and general use of particular forms.

Sometimes native speakers are unclear about the status of a particular structure. Some native speakers would never say *He ought not to have done it, ought he* always preferring *He shouldn't have done that, should he.* Some speakers seem to have a choice between *ought* and *should,* while for others there is either a different choice, or no choice at all.

Sometimes, ironically, education interferes with the natural choice. Some years ago I asked a number of native speakers who work in offices to complete the spaces in the sentences below saying whether they thought:

> that *would* was possible, but *should* was not
> that *should* was possible, but *would* was not
> that both were possible

1. *We . . . be delighted to ask our representative to call.*
2. *We . . . like once more to apologise for the inconvenience you have been caused.*
3. *We . . . be grateful if you could despatch the order by return.*
4. *The work . . . take about 3 months if we are able to start on the 1st of April.*
5. *We . . . be grateful if you . . . pass on this information to your client.*

The sample was too small to draw any firm conclusions, but one thing did emerge — native speakers were fairly confused! For each question a significant number of people voted for each of the three possible answers. The last example caused particular problems. Quite a large number of people said that they had learned the "rule" that they must not use the same word twice in a sentence. These people automatically voted for either *should/would* or *would/should.* Other people asked themselves "which one sounded best". Some relied on intuition, others on what they had learnt. Not surprisingly, they produced different answers.

We can never be sure that the range of choices available to each speaker is the same. We can never be sure why the speaker has made a particular choice. Despite these difficulties, we need to recognise that the speaker does make choices, and that grammar is not only a matter of objective fact.

This has implications for the classroom. Teachers will be familiar with exercises of the type *Put the verb given in either the present simple or present continuous in the following examples.* Some examples can be constructed which are unambiguous. This is always the case with grammar as fact. In many more examples, however, two well-formed sentences will be possible with slightly different meanings. Such practices are dangerous in that they subconsciously suggest to both teachers and students that all grammar is grammar as fact. If a book contains only such practices, grammar as choice and exploration of the semantics of different forms are totally ignored.

Basic meaning and contextual use

The Principle of General Use discussed in Chapter 4 suggested that all uses of a particular form share certain characteristics of meaning. In this chapter we have seen that communicative meaning is a combination of the fundamental semantics and factors such as expectation and environment. It is obvious that if we are to look at the fundamental semantics, these cannot be found by interpreting particular examples in individual contexts. An example makes this clear. In a certain context the speaker may say *He left when I came in.* A listener may well interpret this as suggesting causality (He left *because* I came in). In context that may be the communicative meaning. It cannot, however, be the general explanation of the forms the speakers used. There is no necessary causal connection in the structurally similar sentence *He put the car in the garage when I arrived.*

One particular group of explanations based on interpretation may easily cause confusion. It is not uncommon to tell students that " . . . is more polite than . . .". What does the contrast *polite/impolite* mean? What is considered perfectly polite in one situation may be considered impolite in another. It is not difficult to think of two couples struggling with heavy suitcases, where for one couple *Give us a hand with this can you?* is appropriate, while the other would say *Excuse me, I wonder if you'd mind helping me with this please.*

The second is more formal and less intimate: it would be appropriate between two strangers. The first would be inappropriate between two strangers and, if used in that situation would be thought "impolite". Equally, the second used between two teenage hitchhikers who knew each other, while not "impolite" would almost certainly prompt the question *What's wrong with you?*

"Politeness" is to do with the fact that the speaker tries to conform in certain ways to the listener's expectations. The young hitchhiker is unlikely to think his friend has been impolite; what was said conformed to the hearer's expectation and was, therefore, in no way impolite.

Students are sometimes told: Use "some" in polite offers as in *Would you like some tea.* But the speaker does not choose *some* in such examples in order to "be polite". It is the semantic difference between *some* and *any* which determines the choice. If *some* is associated with so-called polite offers the reason for this can be understood. Explanations based on "politeness" ignore the underlying question of the meaning of the forms used. For this reason they are not, in fact, explanations of the forms.

Interpretive explanations of particular examples can easily lead to confusion about the general meaning. It is the primary distinctions of meaning which combine with other factors to create the communicative meaning. It is these primary semantic distinctions which are discussed in Chapters 8 to 15.

6. Time, Tense, Aspect, Mood.

The term "tense" is frequently used loosely. It is often used to mean no more than different forms of the verb. Traditionally, grammarians use different terms to describe different kinds of verbal construction. As we shall see, some of these traditional distinctions are very helpful in understanding the basic structure of the verb. First, however, one particularly important distinction needs to be made.

Time and Tense

Time is not the same thing as tense. The importance of the distinction cannot be overestimated. Time is an element of our experience of reality. Tense is a purely grammatical idea.

We have already noted that the task of the grammarian is to collect and sort examples which reveal patterns. The procedure often involves sorting the examples into different categories. There may be no simple explanation of the difference between the categories, it simply being a matter that certain language items behave in a partiuclar way, and others in a different way. It is, for example, common to refer to nouns in many European languages as "masculine" and "feminine". It is essential to understand that this has *nothing to do with sex* — female persons may perform functions which are identified by so-called "masculine" nouns or vice versa; impersonal objects are grammatically categorised as "masculine" or "femine". It is even possible for the same object to be referred to by two different nouns, one of which is masculine and the other of which is feminine — in French, for example, a particular school may be referred to as a school — *l'école,* which is feminine, but if referred to by the type of school, *un lycée,* it will be masculine. The confusion in this case comes from the names of the categories — masculine and feminine. If they were referred to as Group 1 and Group 2 nouns, the difference would be less surprising. Membership of the group simply means a particular noun shares certain grammatical characteristics with other nouns in that group.

A similar confusion arises when we think of tenses. It is easy to think of the present tense having something to do with present time, or the past tense with past time. Examples soon show us that this is not true:

Examples	Comment
I speak quite good French.	Refers to general, not present time.
We leave at 4 o'clock tomorrow.	Present tense, future time.
Would you mind if I opened the window?	Past tense, present or future time.
Have you ever been there before?	Past time but without the past tense.

There are many more examples where the grammatical tense and the time referred to are not the same. (See the list on page 38)

Real Time

Most people probably feel that they share the same idea of time. According to our normal perception, time is divided into Past, Present and Future. In this book, we refer to the exact moment of speaking as "the point Now". Then, in an obvious sense, Past Time is time before Now; Future Time is time after Now. Present Time is all that is left — that is simply the *point* Now.

In real time there is no such thing as "a present period" — by definition a period must extend in time, and therefore cannot be wholly "in" Present Time.

It is difficult to remember that we have learnt our idea of time. Anyone who has told a small child *Not now, later,* will soon understand, however, that up to a certain age children have no idea what *later* means.

Different kinds of Time

We have already seen that tense and time do not correspond directly. Even so, we have a strong feeling that the use of different verb forms has *something* to do with ideas of time. It is helpful, therefore, before we think about the meaning of particular grammatical forms in English, to ask ourselves what kind of distinctions *might* be possible. If we think of the English pronoun system we see, for example, that it is possible to distinguish the speaker *I,* from the listener *you,* the personal *he/she,* from the impersonal *it,* the involvement of the speaker, *I/we,* from the non-involvement of the speaker, etc. But it is easy to think of other distinctions which could be possible. For example, English *we* means "the speaker and one or more other people", but it would be quite possible to have different pronouns for, for example,
1. the speaker and the listener
2. the speaker and somebody else, not the listener
3. the speaker and more than one other person.

By thinking of the distinctions which *could* be made, rather than those which we know *are* made, we can to some extent clear our minds of our preconceptions. At this point, therefore, readers are invited to ask themselves how time can be divided into "different kinds of time". Try to make as long a list as possible with distinctions which you can conceptualise, even if you do not think they are realised in the verb system of either English, or your own language. In fact, of course, many more possible distinctions exist than are actually made directly in the verbal system of our languages. It is surprising how difficult it is to think of different kinds of time which are not directly related to how we think the verb system works, but it is possible and a useful exercise. Some possible distinctions are given below.

a. Perhaps the simplest of all temporal distinctions is *Now* versus *not-Now,* which we could perhaps call *Then.*
b. We could imagine that it would be possible and useful to distinguish *real* time from *imaginary* time — this would mean fiction and the future would use one form, while statements about the past and now would use another.

c. We could distinguish *finished* and *unfinished* actions.

d. It might be useful to distinguish *unique* events from *repeated* events.

e. We have already noted that in our normal understanding of time, the point Now naturally divides time into two — *Before Now,* and *After Now.*

f. We could divide time into those events or states which include the point Now, contrasted with those which do not include that point.

So far all of these distinctions have been dichotomies — they have divided things into *two* parts. In some ways this is rather strange, as what we usually think of as the natural division of time is into three — Past, Present, Future. We have, however, already noted the difficulty which this tri-partite division raises. 'Now' is essentially a *point* in time, an instant with no duration. If events are to happen *in* time, we must think of *periods,* not points.

So far, all we have done is to list possible contrasts in the idea of time. With this last distinction, however, we have met an idea which is of considerable practical importance. We need to ask whether we are talking about real, objective time, or what we might perhaps call psychological time. This distinction is of great importance. Objectively speaking, any event which happens takes a certain length of time. The length of time may be very short, but nothing happens instantaneously. On the other hand it is quite common for us to perceive things as if they happened instantaneously: *The phone rang at exactly ten past three.*

From the point of view of the language we use, it is clearly the psychological time, the way we perceive the action, which is important, not what "objectively happened". We have here the first clue to the central, and very important idea discussed in the previous chapter. We may state it very simply as we cannot analyse the language a person uses independently of that person's perception of what happened.

Some years ago language teaching was usually based on a structuralist approach; students studied different structures in sequence. More recently, the idea of a notional/functional approach has been much more popular. A function may be defined as what the speaker is doing with the language at a particular time; most readers will be familiar with such headings as *refusing permission* and *asking for information,* from their textbooks. As far as time is concerned, two obvious functions are *asking* and *telling the time.* Both of these are dealt with in textbooks and involve a very limited range of words and structures. But what, on the other hand, of the *notion* of time? I have never seen a language teaching textbook which attempts to discuss this, at least not systematically and coherently. A discussion of this notion would involve such ideas as how we express the difference between completeness and incompleteness, point and period, simultaneous and successive events, the similarities and differences between Then (past) and Then (future). In short, a discussion of the notion of time involves the kind of exploration we are considering, what kinds of time may be conceived, and how these different kinds of time can be expressed in words? Are the different kinds of time and temporal relationships expressed through the use of structures, or through the use of lexical items *(adverbials)*?

This question may appear abstract, but it is impossible to approach understanding the difference between, for example, the present perfect and the past simple without considering the underlying question, which is the different ways Past Time may be perceived. (This is discussed in Chapters 9 and 10).

A task for the reader

Most people would agree that we may perceive events either as points in time, or as periods in time: *I turned the light off; We were waiting nearly half an hour.*

It is also not difficult to imagine the difference between definitely limited periods *(We were waiting nearly half and hour),* and more "open ended" periods *(I live in London).*

It is also easy to see that points and periods may be at different places in time. If we draw a line to represent time, and mark the present moment by the point Now:

we can represent different kinds of events with diagrams. Here are two examples:

The reader will find it very helpful to experiment with such drawings. See how many different drawings you can make. Think of the difference between points and periods, whether the period ends or not, where the points or ends of the periods are. You should be able to make at least a dozen different diagrams. When you have tried, you will find more examples on page 54.

Tense

To the linguist tense is a technical term. It means that there is a morphological change in the base form of the verb. A verb form which is made with an auxiliary is not, in this technical meaning, a "tense".

In this technical sense, then, English verbs have only two tenses, those traditionally called the Present Simple *(go)* and the Past Simple *(went).* All other forms are made using auxiliaries, in particular the auxiliaries **(be)** and **(have).**

The first interesting feature of this distinction is that English does not have a Future Tense. This, of course, does not mean that it is not possible to talk about Future Time in English, but that there is no one verb form specifically, or even strongly, associated with Future Time. On a practical level teachers are often familiar with this problem. The choice of the correct form of the verb for different situations to refer to Future Time in English, is often a major problem for students. Explaining the difference between the different usages is often a major problem for teachers. But as we shall see, the purely technical information that English does not possess a future tense, will, in due course, help us to understand some of the practical problems associated with explaining the different verb forms which are used to refer to Future Time.

We have already met examples of the present tense, which do not refer to Present Time, and examples of the past tense which do not refer to Past Time. We have now established that there is no future tense, and already know that the present tense may be used to refer to Future Time. It begins to look as if the situation is becoming more and more complicated. It may also appear as if the theoretical distinctions are little more than an intellectual game. This is very far from the case. We have two important facts — we think of Time as dividing into three, Past, Present and Future, but we have only two Tenses; secondly, it is not possible to make a direct association between present tense and Present Time, or between past tense and Past Time. These two facts suggest a most important idea — is it possible the fundamental, underlying distinction between the use of the present tense and the past tense is *not* neatly associated with Time? However much we may intuitively feel that time and tense are linked, is it possible that association with Past Time is not a defining characteristic of the past tense, and association with Present Time is not a defining characteristic of the present tense? This surprising idea is, in fact, true and of immense help in understanding the most fundamental distinction in the English verb, discussed in detail on pages 66/67.

Readers may like to be reassured on one point — to a linguist it is not surprising that English has no Future Tense. Providing we have the distinction between tense and time clearly in our minds this is not surprising. After all, Russian has no articles, and Finnish has no prepositions. Those kinds of relationships are expressed in different ways in those languages. Different languages have evolved in different ways so that a grammatical distinction which exists in one may exist, not exist, or exist in quite a different way, in another. This should neither surprise nor worry us.

Aspect

In addition to the verb forms which a linguist regards as tenses, there are many other forms in English. These other forms are made with auxiliaries:

He'*s* learn*ing* French.
We'*ve been* there before.
You could *have* ask*ed* me first.
He must *have been* try*ing* to ring you.

These forms include what a grammarian would call *aspect*. For our purposes we may define this as a verb form involving the use of an auxiliary which allows the speaker to *interpret the temporal elements of an event.*

This area will be explored in much more detail in Chapters 10 to 12 when we look at verb forms made with the auxiliaries *(have), (be)* and *(be) + going to.* For the moment we may observe that a pure tense form is used to give what the speaker sees as the "bald facts" of the situation. The auxiliaries provide greater insight into the speaker's interpretation of the temporal aspects. In one sense *I last met him three months ago* and *I haven't seen him for three months* "have the same meaning". There are, however, various reasons why the speaker chooses one form rather than the other. Aspect gives the speaker the opportunity to interpret the temporal nature of the action — whether it is complete or incomplete, the time-orientation of an action, or the fact that the action concerned a finite period of time. Once again we shall find that different languages have aspects but it is not possible to make the aspectual system of one language fit that of another language.

Mood

Auxiliaries are used to make aspectual forms — *I've rung him; They're playing in the garden,* but not all auxiliaries are used for this purpose. There is a whole group in English, called the modal auxiliaries (see Chapters 13 and 14), which allow the speaker to interpret the non-factual and non-temporal elements in an event. Modal auxiliaries are one way for a speaker to introduce *modality* into what (s)he says. Modality includes such ideas as necessity, possibility, probability etc. Large books have been written on the English modal auxiliaries. Here we are only concerned to establish a working definition — modality allows the speaker to introduce a *personal interpretation of the non-factual and non-temporal* elements of the event.

It is possible to see the construction of a verb form as a sequence:

Reality	Speaker's Pre-knowledge	Speaker's Interpretation			Listener's Pre-knowledge	Listener's Interpretation
		of Factuality	of Temporal Features	Judgement of Non-Factuality		
		(Tense)	(Aspect)	(Mood)		

A speaker decides *what* (s)he wishes to talk about and chooses the basic words. In the case of a verb the basic (infinitive) form is appropriate. This may be sufficient to convey a whole message with, for example, signs which say PUSH or PULL. *Who* is to push or *when* are unnecessary questions.

Usually, of course, the speaker will wish, or need, to tell us *who* performs the action. This will introduce 'a subject' for the verb. Sometimes that is sufficient; if I say *I understand,* a complete message is conveyed.

In English, though not necessarily in other languages, the speaker has a choice of seeing the *facts* of the situation in *two* ways. Depending on which of those two (s)he chooses, one or other of the two tense forms will be appropriate.

More often than not, the speaker will wish to provide a temporal interpretation of the action. In these cases certain auxiliaries introduce aspect.

If the speaker also wishes to express a personal judgement about the non-factual nature of the event, a modal auxiliary can be used.

I am not suggesting that this is a conscious process, nor that the speaker follows a strict sequence even unconsciously. The point is simpler than that — certain elements of the structure of a complex verb form are used in certain *regular* ways. By recognising those regularities, it is easier to understand both the structure and meaning of complex verb forms.

The distinctions discussed in this chapter are those made by linguists, but teachers will find it easier to understand the meaning of different verb forms if the distinctions are borne in mind.

Summary

In understanding the semantics of English verb forms, the most important insight is that those forms traditionally called "present simple" and "past simple", are used when the speaker wishes to offer a non-temporal statement of the situation. This is so at variance with traditional thinking that it can seem confusing or unhelpful. Nothing could be further from the truth. All forms other than these two pure tense forms offer some form of speaker interpretation; the pure tense forms are not interpretive. They describe what the speaker sees as pure factuality. The essential characteristic of the use of the forms is that the speaker conceptualises the event described by such a form as undivided, or unitary. This idea is discussed further on page 94. This "self-containedness" is not essentially temporal. In contrast, ideas of time are intrinsic to forms which are aspectual. In English this means those forms traditionally called "perfect" or "continuous". The temporal interpretation of these forms is discussed respectively in Chapters 10 and 12.

From the classroom point of view, it is important to recognise that it is a mistake to introduce *will/shall* (or, indeed any other form) as "the future" in English. The problem of the expression of Future Time is discussed in considerable detail in Chapters 8, 12, 14 and 17. As will be seen from this long list, it is a complex area. To ensure a clear understanding, it is essential to start by establishing that no one verb form in English has a central role as "the future".

Terminology in the classroom

If students meet terms such as "present tense" and "past tense", it is perhaps inevitable that they will confuse these with Present Time and Past Time. Unfortunately, the majority of books continue to use these forms. Teachers may care to consider whether the greatly simplified terminology which is suggested in Chapter 20 would help them to avoid confusion.

Here are some examples of the kinds of time drawings we can make. At this point these are only *possible* drawings. Later we shall find some of these are reflected in the structure of the English verb and others are not.

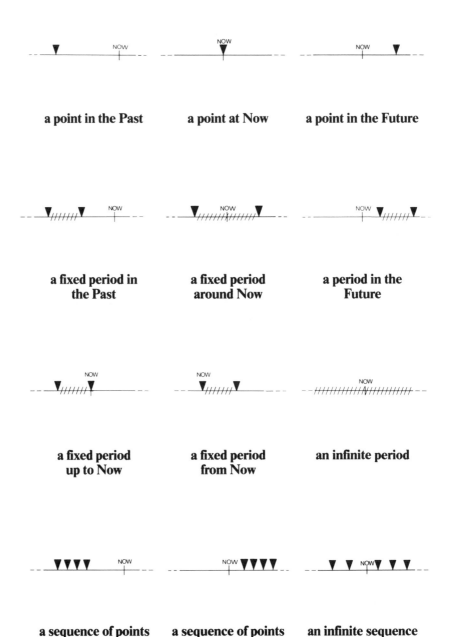

a point in the Past	**a point at Now**	**a point in the Future**
a fixed period in the Past	**a fixed period around Now**	**a period in the Future**
a fixed period up to Now	**a fixed period from Now**	**an infinite period**
a sequence of points in the Past	**a sequence of points in the Future**	**an infinite sequence of points**

There is a discussion of the uses and dangers of time-line drawings applied to English verb forms on pages 170 to 175.

7. Auxiliary Patterns

We turn our attention now to the analysis of different forms of the English verb. For this purpose the basic 'unit' is the verb phrase of a clause, not, for example, the sequence of verb phrases which we may find in a full sentence.

Operators

There is one further distinction we need to make before beginning the analysis of different forms. In subsequent chapters we will concentrate on the meanings associated with the different forms and auxiliaries. Certain elements of meaning, however, are conveyed in English by *manipulating* the verb form, for example, the formation of negatives and questions.

Loosely, a positive statement may be made negative by "adding *not*". An accurate satement needs to be more precise — where is the *not* to be added? The answer is immediately after the *first* auxiliary of the verb phrase, joining to that auxiliary (as *n't*) if unstressed:

> *He can't come after all.*
> *We haven't done anything about it yet.*
> *They mustn't have arrived yet.*

In a similar way the question form may be made from the statement form by changing the order of the subject and the *first* auxiliary.

> *Have you heard yet?*
> *Were you going to watch it?*
> *Could it still be in the office?*

In examples such as these we see that the first auxiliary has two roles in the sentence:
(i)   It adds its usual meaning (discussed in the following Chapters).
(ii) It acts as an *operator* so that, for example, by changing its position in the sentence, the meaning is changed.

The Dummy Auxiliary

The manner in which operators work in English is extremely general. The descriptive rules are *always* followed. At first sight it appears that such sentences as:

> *Did he take the 4.30?*
> *I didn't know you'd been there.*

do not follow the rule. In fact, they do, providing those rules are stated more precisely. The formal statement is as follows:

> Where the verb phrase has no auxiliary in the positive declarative
> sentence, *(do)* is introduced when an operator is required.

This rule, which introduces an extraordinary regularity into the English
verb, may be expanded as follows:

> If a particular pattern — of structure or stress — is made using
> an auxiliary, that pattern is preserved for *all* English verb
> phrases which do not contain an auxiliary by introducing part
> of *(do)* as a "dummy auxiliary". The patterns are then fol-
> lowed without exception.

Textbooks and teachers frequently present *(do)* as if it were an
irregularity. It is common to refer to "questions with do" or, for example, to
present and practise tags in sentences with an auxiliary on one occasion,
and those without an auxiliary, requiring part of *(do)* on another. There may
be good pedagogical reasons for doing this. There is, however, frequently a
side-effect — students believe that one pattern is valid on one occasion and
on other occasions a *different* pattern is used. This is not the case, but the
regularity of the language has been obscured by the presentation.

It is still not unusual for even the most modern foreign grammars of
English to present "the (do) construction" as a separate chapter, and exception. A certain well-known British-produced reference book contains these
lines:

> *Did Peter enjoy the party?*
> *Did you all go straight home afterwards?*
> In all other tenses we form the interrogative by putting
> the subject after the auxiliary:
> *Have you finished?   Are they coming?*

The same book referring to negatives says:

> All other tenses are formed with auxiliaries, and the
> negative is formed by putting *not* after the auxiliary.

You will notice that the first examples have the subject immediately after
an auxiliary, *did,* but the book phrases its description in such a way as to
suggest that "all other tenses" are different. In fact all behave the same. The
same comment applies to the formation of negatives.

Knowing the formal identity of rules for questions and negatives will not
necessarily help students to make fewer mistakes when they produce the
language naturally and spontaneously. It does, however, present a simpler,
more coherent and more accurate picture of how English verb forms work.

Regular Patterns

(Do) is used as the dummy auxiliary in all patterns, of structure or stress,
which normally depend upon the use of the first auxiliary as operator. A list
of the most important uses of this kind is given below. Two points are to be
noted — the regularity introduced into the language through the use of *(do)*
as dummy auxiliary, and the patterns themselves in which the auxiliary is
used as operator.

1. Making a Negative

Rule: add *n't* to the end of the first auxiliary.

He can swim.	→*He can't swim.*
They have gone.	→ *They haven't gone.*

If there is no auxiliary use **(do)** and follow the pattern in the same way.

He goes often.	→*He doesn't go often.*
He went yesterday.	→ *He didn't go yesterday.*

2. Forming a Question

Rule: change the order of the subject and the first auxiliary.

He can swim.	→*Can he swim?*
They could have left.	→*Could they have left?*

If there is no auxiliary, use **(do)** and follow the same pattern.

He goes often.	→*Does he go often?*
He went yesterday.	→*Did he go yesterday?*

3. Emphasis

Rule: give the auxiliary its full, stressed, form.

They're waiting.	→ *They are waiting.*

If there is no auxiliary, introduce **(do)** and follow the same pattern.

I think you should.	→*I do think you should.*
I waited an hour.	→*I did wait an hour.*

4. Making a tag (1) — To invite a response (See Chapter 18)

Rule: positive sentences have negative tags; negative sentences have positive tags. Use the first auxiliary in the tag.

He can swim.	→*He can swim, can't he.*
He must have left.	→*He must have left, mustn't he.*

If there is no auxiliary, use **(do)** and follow the same pattern.

He knows her.	→*He knows her, doesn't he.*
They went.	→ *They went, didn't they.*

5. Making a tag (2) — To show surprise or annoyance (See Chapter 18)

Rule: positive sentences have positive tags, negative sentences have negative tags. Use the first auxiliary.

You've met before.	→ *You've met before, have you!*
You can't do it.	→ *You can't do it, can't you!*

If there is no auxiliary, use **(do)** and follow the same pattern.

You two know each other.	→ *You two know each other, do you!*
You warned me.	→ *You warned me, did you!*

6. Making an "interested response"

Rule: the second speaker uses the appropriate form of the first auxiliary in what is said by the first speaker:

A *I've been there before.*   **A** *I'd be very surprised.*
B *Have you?*   **B** *Would you?*

If there is no auxiliary, use **(do)** and follow the same pattern.

A *I know them well.*   **A** *I saw them yesterday.*
B *Do you?*   **B** *Did you?*

7. Making an agreement response

Rule: the second speaker uses the appropriate form of the first auxiliary used by the first speaker:

A *Have you been there before?*   **A** *Can you speak French?*
B *Yes I have.*   **B** *Yes I can.*
   No I haven't.   *No I can't.*

(do) follows the same pattern.

A *Do you know where it is?*   **A** *Did you post that letter?*
B *Yes I do.*   **B** *Yes I did.*
   No I don't.   *No I didn't.*

The following examples are also similar:

A *I can make Saturday.*   **A** *I was going to tell her.*
B *Yes, so can I.*   **B** *Yes, so was I.*

A *I can't understand.*   **A** *I won't be there.*
B *No, neither can I.*   **B** *No, neither will I.*

A *I enjoyed that.*   **A** *We need a holiday.*
B *Yes, so did I.*   **B** *Yes, so do I.*

A *I don't like winter.*   **A** *He didn't like it.*
B *No, neither do I.*   **B** *No, neither did we.*

These examples make clear the important role of the first auxiliary in the English verb. They also emphasise the role of the dummy auxiliary, **(do)**, in ensuring great regularity in verb patterns.

A number of small points need to be made:

1. The verbs **(be)** and **(have)** may be used as operators when used as main verbs as well as when used as auxiliaries:

He's late.   *Is he late?*
They were there.   *They were there, weren't they?*
He has some money.   *He hasn't any money.*
They have three children.   *Have they any children?*

2. Not all inversions are questions. The following constructions, although infrequent, are still found in contemporary English (See Chapter 19)

Were you to ask him, I doubt if he would agree.
Had you been insured, the problem would not have been so serious.
Should he need help, please tell him to get in touch with me.

3. From a classroom point of view it is important to note that the general rule for negation (add *n't* to the first auxiliary) produces two anomalies:

> English has no form **willn't* and students need to learn the form *won't*. There is no form **amn't*.

All these points may be summarized by one very general and very powerful rule:
(Do) is not an irregular feature of English, it is the feature which preserves regularity. It is valuable to draw students' attention to this.

In the classroom

Attention has already been drawn elsewhere to the unfortunate practice of emphasising irregularity rather than regularity. There is something remarkably reassuring about the fact that the patterns described in this chapter are so general, so regular and powerful. It is particularly difficult for teachers to avoid emphasising difference rather than similarity if the grammar book they are using presents patterns containing the dummy auxiliary first and then treats forms containing other auxiliaries later. It is considerably easier to *start* with forms containing auxiliaries and show that, by the introduction of **(do)** as a dummy, the patterns are preserved.

It is clear that, in the classroom, if one practice is done with sentences which contain an auxiliary, then one with those using **(do)** as the dummy auxiliary, a third practice is necessary in which examples of both kinds are presented. This serves two purposes: to draw the students' attention to the one single underlying pattern, and to develop fluency in *using* the forms (as opposed to an *understanding* of their use). The teaching sequence best suited to developing fluency will include this third, discrimination, practice.

The importance of the auxiliary for the classroom can hardly be over-estimated. Such important characteristics of the spoken language as tags and interested responses, and such important structural characteristics as the formation of question and negative forms depend upon the ability to manipulate the auxiliary, including **(do).**

This means students at all stages of the course require practice not only from a productive, but from a receptive point of view. Frequently the auxiliary is reduced to **'s** and this may represent *is* or *has;* **'d** may represent *had* or *would*. Clearly if students are to respond they need to hear, recognise and be able to identify accurately these forms in the stream of speech. Many students who have a relatively good knowledge of written English, and of certain structural features of English, find informal conversation difficult precisely because they do not have sufficient facility in the manipulation of the auxiliary. Teachers need to emphasise it in relation to the different skills, and *throughout* the course, not just in the early stages.

8. The First Form of the Verb

Verbs in many European languages possess a form often referred to as the base form. It is the 'stem' to which various endings are added to indicate, for example, different tenses or persons. This idea, if carried over into English, is ridiculous. The base form of the English verb *walk* is *walk*. The form usually called the infinitive (without *to*) is identical with the base form. The only endings which may be added to the base form are *-s, -ing* and *-ed*. This contrasts with the enormous number of endings possible in, for example, French or Italian.

The concept of the base form is, therefore, not particularly useful in English. Because the infinitive and base forms are identical, however, a form exists which may conveniently be referred to as *the basic form*.

Seen through the eyes of traditional terminology and categories, the basic form appears to have a catalogue of uses. Further examination shows that these apparently different uses share certain important features of meaning. This in turn means the idea of a *basic* form is useful.

This basic form is used for what are traditionally called the infinitive, the imperative, and the present simple (with the historical anomaly of the third person **-s.** Can the fact that one form fulfils all these roles be explained reasonably? How are they similar? What are the identifying shared characteristics?

Earlier, we saw speakers constructing verb forms through a series of choices; additional elements within the verb phrase added the speaker's interpretation. The complete message is sometimes conveyed by a single word. The verb form which is appropriate to these single word messages is, as we would expect, the basic form.

There is an important sense in which we cannot ask *Why is the basic form used?* It is the form which is appropriate when no special interpretation is intended by the speaker. As we shall see in subsequent chapters each other form adds specific meaning; the basic form is appropriate when none of those specific additional meanings are required by the speaker. This explanation applies to all the superficially different "uses" of the basic form.

The Infinitive

Traditionally this is the basic form of the verb. It is the form which is listed in dictionaries and grammar books and the form which is given first in tables of principal parts:

take took taken
bring brought brought

The Imperative

This term has been adopted from Latin grammar. Latin, like many modern European languages, has a distinct form for this use; English does not. If native English speakers are asked *What is the imperative?* the most frequent reply is *The form used to give orders.* This answer is not satisfactory from a grammatical point of view. Firstly, the form is not used uniquely for this purpose:

Come in and take your coat off.
Take two eggs, break them into a bowl and beat thoroughly.

These are not orders, but an *invitation* and an *instruction.*
Nor is it true that orders are always given with "the imperative":

Will you be quiet!
Would you open the door please.

may on occasions be "orders".

There is no one-to-one correspondence between form and function. It would be remarkable if English possessed a form which was identified with the discourse function *Giving orders;* it would be the *only* English verb form identified with a specific discourse function.

The problem of "explaining the use of the imperative" presupposes the existence of a form which is "the imperative". It is not possible to identify a form which has this function, nor a function which is uniquely identified with the form. The logical conclusion is that English does not have "an imperative".

We have already seen that when the whole message is conveyed by the use of the basic form, that is precisely the form which is used. If the questions of *who* and *when* (the temporal restrictions) are irrelevant, the basic form is appropriate. The questions of *who* or *when* will be irrelevant when they are self-evident from the circumstances — either because they are generally applicable, as with the case of instructions:

Press button to start.
Bring to the boil and simmer for 20 minutes.

or because it is the person or people addressed who are to perform the action at an "obvious" time, usually the moment of speaking. This case usually applies to genuine orders (where the hearer accepts the authority of the speaker) and invitations:

Take aim, fire!
Fetch, boy, fetch (said to a dog!).
Help yourself. Don't wait for me.

In all of these cases the questions of *who* and *when* are absurd — all that matters is *what;* the communication is complete once the speaker has identified the *what,* using the basic form.

The Present Simple

It is not, of course, true that "the present" simple" is identical with the basic form of the verb. In the third person the **-s** form is required. There are historical reasons for this, and though causing no difficulty of understanding, it often causes problems for both teachers and students. The present simple in all other persons, however, *is* identical with the basic form of the verb. Can this usage be explained in a consistent and coherent way? Does the use which appears to be "the present simple" have characteristics in common with the use of the basic form which we have already discussed?

We may identify six apparently different common uses of the form:

(1) *I pronounce you man and wife.*
(2) *I take three eggs . . . I break them into a bowl . . .*
(3) *Wood floats on water.*
(4) *I play tennis regularly.*
(5) *I'll ask him when I see him.*
(6) *We leave from Paddington tomorrow morning at 7.30.*

At first sight these uses appear to have little in common with each other, nor with uses of the basic form so far discussed. In fact, they all share important characteristics.

(1) I pronounce you man and wife.

This usage is restricted to certain verbs — I shall call them *declarative verbs* — in which the saying of the sentence is the action described by the sentence. Further examples are:

I swear by almighty God ...(the oath taken in court).
That's all right, I forgive you.

We have already seen that we may divide time into Past Time, Present Time, and Future Time. Although all actions are in reality somewhat extended in time, the speaker conceptualises these actions, using declarative verbs, as coincident with the point Now; in a completely literal sense these are *present* uses of the form. It would be absurd to ask the question *when* about these examples — the answer would be *Now, of course, when do you think!*

The whole message is not, however, now conveyed by 'what' — there is a difference between *I forgive you* and *We forgive you*. A subject is needed but, as we would expect, the answer to the question *'who'* together with the basic form conveys the whole message, so that verb form is appropriate.

(2) I take three eggs . . . I break them into a bowl . . .

The 'commentary' use is similar. The speaker conveys the whole message by answering the questions *who* and *what*. The *when* question — *on what occasion* (or perhaps *under what restriction?*) is not appropriate — the answer would be *Now, of course.*

This form is well known as characteristic of certain sports commentaries, where the speaker (commentator) sees a sequence of punctual single-entity actions. It is *not* used for 'background' remarks (see page 96). *Connors serves to the left-hand court, Lendl on the backhand hits the ball into the net.*

(3) Wood floats on water.

Such sentences are associated with general statements or "eternal truths":

Water freezes at 32°F.   *God loves us.*

These are in no way associated with the moment of speaking, Now. This may suggest that the form has two uses — for punctual events at Now, and for 'timeless' events or states. In fact, there is an underlying unity of meaning — in *both* cases time reference is unnecessary. With examples such as (3) the answer to the question *On what occasion?* is *Always, of course.*

It is interesting to note that the absurdity of the question *On what occasion?* is reflected in the use of *Of course* in the answer. That is the clue to why the basic form is appropriate.

(4) I play tennis regularly.

This example relates not to a single occasion but to many occasions. Teachers frequently describe this use as associated with repeated or habitual actions. Such a description is accurate, but notice that such examples also have something in common with those already listed. The question *On what occasion?* — note carefully the singular, *occasion* not *occasions* — is inappropriate, or even absurd.

In Chapter 6 we noted that it may be of interest to distinguish single from repeated actions. We now notice that English does not make this distinction through choice of verb form. The basic form of the verb may be appropriate to a single punctual, action *(I propose a toast)* or a series of actions *(I play tennis regularly)* or a single but extended action *(I live in Oxford, He speaks very good German)*. We saw that many distinctions were possible, but now we also see that it is *not* characteristic of the present simple that it is associated with Present Time; the feature which all uses of the present simple share is that temporal reference is unnecessary. (The contrasts with examples containing reference to time or temporal interpretation — *I'm living in Oxford, I'm playing the piano.* — are discussed in Chapter 12).

(5) I'll ask him when I see him.

The basic form of the verb is appropriate to general statements such as (3); temporal restriction does not apply. It is easy to see then, by generalising, that the form is also appropriate to clauses beginning with *if,* *when,* and other similar words. In the example given, the occasion to which the speaker refers is apparent; once again, the question *when* is inappropriate.

(6) We leave from Paddington at 7.30 tomorrow morning.

This use appears more difficult to explain. It is the use often referred to as "the present simple used for the future". The example seems to have a specific time reference — *at 7.30 tomorrow morning.* This is deceptive. It is easy to see that the uses of *leave* in *We leave from Paddington* and *We leave at 7.30 tomorrow morning* are identical. The first one does not contain a specific time reference, although the second does. The conclusion we must draw is that the time reference is a coincidence, not an intrinsic feature of the use of the verb form. The explanation is surprisingly simple. The basic form of the verb with a subject — what we usually think of as the present simple — is appropriate to all statements which, at the moment of speaking, the speaker sees as *facts*. In Chapter 17 we discuss the reasons which influence the speaker in selecting a particlar verb form to talk about Future Time. Here, however, we may observe that the same verb form is appropriate to all of the following:

Paris is the capital of France.
It's my birthday next Tuesday.
We leave at 7.30 tomorrow morning.

The first two statements are, objectively speaking, facts. But we noted in Chapter 5 that language is more personal and subjective than is sometimes recognised. The speaker uses language to describe his or her perception of a situation. The speaker will describe a future event using the basic form of the verb if, at the moment of speaking, the speaker sees the future event as a matter of factual certainty. It is easy to see that this will be the case if, for example, the speaker is basing the statement on the perception of information coming from an outside *force majeur.*

In cases such as (1), (2), (3) and (4), it can appear that the essential characteristic of the use of the basic form of the verb is lack of temporal reference. This, however, overlooks the fact that it is lack of temporal reference *from the speaker's point of view.* Explicit time reference is possible: *I play tennis every Saturday in the winter.*
and with reference to Future Time specific time reference is possible:
Arsenal play away on Saturday:
but in the latter case the speaker feels the event is certain to take place because it is totally outside the control of the speaker so, *to that person,* it has the same timeless quality as: *Christmas Day falls on a Thursday this year.*

An unmarked form

We have seen that the basic form of the verb is appropriate to answer the question *what.* If the answer to the question conveys the speaker's whole message, the basic form is used alone: *Help! Wait for me!* When the questions *who* and *what* are appropriate, the basic form will be used in sentences usually thought of as "the present simple".

All of these uses have in common that questions of restriction are *not* appropriate — questions such as *When? On what occasion?* or, *Under what restrictions?* When none of these temporal questions is appropriate, the verb form will be the basic form.

This explanation may seem curiously negative — the basic form is used when certain conditions are *not* fulfilled. This is exactly the case, and is theoretically sound. If we wish to know someone's age the natural question is *How old is he? How young is he?* is possible and correct English. It is not, however, the expression used in neutral situations; it would be appropriate only if "youngness" was a matter of particular interest or surprise. The use of *How young is he?* would be exceptional and we could reasonably ask why the speaker said it. Such correct but unusual forms are called *marked forms.* It is *not* possible to explain why a speaker selects an unmarked form. They are the normal forms, used in situations which do *not* require marked forms.

It is helpful to see the basic form of the verb in a similar way — as an unmarked form of the verb. We shall see in the following Chapters that we can explain the *additional* meaning conveyed by all other structural elements of the verb form. The form which is appropriate when the whole message is conveyed without these additional marks which show the speaker's interpretation of the event, is the basic form.

The real nature of the "present simple"

The "present simple" is a source of much confusion. This partly stems from the fact that it is frequently taught in contrast to the "present continuous", where two particular uses — the present continuous for an action going on at the moment of speaking, and the present simple for a regular repeated event — are emphasised. While the two forms are used in this way, neither use represents the primary semantic characteristics of the respective forms.

The essential characteristic of the "present simple" is that it expresses the speaker's view of the event as a *timeless fact*. Paradoxically, not only is the present simple not about Present Time, but it is not about time at all. This is a characteristic which it shares with "the past simple". Each of these forms is "simple" in the sense that the speaker sees the events described as single, simple entities, unities, totalities. The "present simple" and "past simple" contrast with each other in that in the first the speaker sees the event as immediate, and with the "past simple" the event is seen as remote. These are not essentially temporal concepts. What matters, for all uses of the simple tense forms, is that the speaker, at the moment of speaking conceptualises the action described as total, complete. As so often in this book, we find that a relatively unusual use of a form helps make this clear. In a sequence of correspondence in the newspaper, it would be natural to write:

C.B. Stewart (June 4th) misses the point of my earlier letter . . .

In conversation, if I think you have not understood me, I may well say *You've missed the point of what I said.* This is a "present perfect", and associated with Present Time. As we see in Chapter 10, there is a temporal interpretation. In the correspondence column, *misses* conceptualises C.B. Stewart's letter as a whole, and clearly wishes to reply to it. The temporal sequence would not allow us to predict this verb form. I wrote my letter; it was published; C.B. Stewart read it; wrote a reply; this was published; I read that; and replied; that reply was published and is now being read by the reader. When I wrote *misses,* C.B. Stewart's letter had been written quite some time earlier, and I had clearly read it before starting to write my reply; *misses* clearly refers to an event in Past Time. We can either introduce a new and inconvenient section to our grammar book — the Present Simple for the past — or accept that the verb form was not chosen for reasons of temporal (time) reference. This may be surprising — we have a tendency to believe that even if time and tense are not the same, they are at least strongly related — but it is not true of English tenses. The essential characteristics of an event described by a "present simple" verb form are:

— the speaker sees the event as a single, total entity. Temporal references are irrelevant.
— the speaker sees the event as a matter of fact.
— the speaker sees the event as immediate, rather than remote (in which case the "past simple" is chosen).

It is easy to see that the event described by a declarative verb such as *I swear it wasn't me* can be conceptualised as a single entity. In fact, it will be seen as a single "point in time". It is a totality, a simple single entity.

In contrast, *Water boils at 100°C* is not conceived as a single act, but can be conceptualised as expressing a single totality, a simple, general truth. In this case the integrity of the conceptualisation is based on its totality, rather than its punctuality. Simplicity, singleness, existing as a single entity, can have different manifestations. Deep down, the essential shared characteristic is the conceptualisation of the act, or state, as an undivided entity. If this seems a difficult and abstract idea, the reader is advised to reflect on the following examples, and consider how each verb expresses an act or event which is a single undivided entity:

*Now I **see** what you mean.*

*It **belongs** to me.*

*I **know** Peter very well.*

*I usually **drive** to work.*

*We always **have** our holidays in June.*

*He **refuses** to say where he got it.*

*The sale **starts** on Saturday.*

*Oxford **leads** by three lengths as they go under the bridge.*

*Newspapers **print** a lot of rubbish.*

*Love **makes** the world go round.*

It is not easy to find good words to describe the essential semantic characteristics of the "present simple" — *undivided entity, simple whole, totality* — none is completely accurate, nor easily accessible. A difficult, or at least unusual, concept is involved. The best way to master the concept is to be patient, and consider carefully a wide range of examples, such as those above.

We have seen that the two pure tense forms in English are used if the speaker expresses no interest in the temporal quality of the event. The choice of such a form is made because of the nature of the speaker's conceptualisation of the event, without reference to questions such as *When? How long?* This remains true even when sentences contain explicit time adverbials:

Now I see what you mean.
We often go there in Summer
They lived there for thirty years.
I waited more than half an hour for you.

The temporal information is given in the time adverbial; the verb form expresses the speaker's perception of the action as an undivided whole.

It is interesting to examine the language for two, apparently similar, situations. First, the verbal description of this simple problem:

$$\text{If } 3x = 6$$
$$x = 2$$

The natural language to describe this is:
If three x equals six, then x equals two.
The verb form for the conclusion is what is usually called the present simple. It is a pure tense and has neither aspectual or modal auxiliaries. This is exactly what we expect, because the statement *Then x equals two* is a statement of objective fact. It is an abstract, logical statement; the speaker is in no way involved in it.

Compare that with *If she marries him, I'll eat my hat.*

With this example it is not possible to say **If she marries him I eat my hat.* The second part of the statement — the conclusion or consequence, is not a matter of fact, and therefore a pure tense form is not possible. The reason *'ll* is appropriate is discussed in Chapter 14. For the moment we see that the theoretical distinction between a pure tense, and a form made using an auxiliary can help us to identify primary semantic distinctions. The language needed to describe these is in the first case rather surprising. In English, pure tense forms are used for what the speaker sees as objective facts. In forms containing an auxiliary, the speaker is interpreting the facts; we may perhaps call these subjective facts. There is no doubt that the idea of objective and subjective facts is a strange one. Nonetheless a distinction of that kind, even if not described in those words, is intrinsic to our understanding the primary semantic distinctions of the English verb.

Summary

Clearly the term *basic form* is easier for students than the traditional terms. There is no reason why the term cannot replace *infinitive* and *imperative*. It is completely theoretically satisfactory, too, to deal with what is traditionally called "the present simple" as the basic form. In this case, however, there is a practical difficulty. If students know or meet the term "present simple" they may well ask teachers when this form is used. We have seen that "the present simple" is an *unmarked* form. The important feature of unmarked forms is that they are used when extra meaning is *not* required. The reason such forms are used is a negative reason — because extra meaning is *not* needed. This can be confusing to students, who look for a definite, positive explanation. If students are slowly to build up a picture of the importance and use of the basic form, it is important for teachers to avoid the catalogue approach, and doing nothing more than giving simple explanations of particular cases. Practices which may lead to deeper understanding are discussed in Chapter 21.

We noted earlier that English had only two tense forms, those usually called present simple and past simple. There was no future tense. Now we have a further surprise — the form traditionally thought of as the present simple can be identified with the basic form. These two bits of information raise a challenging question. We cannot identify the dichotomous tenses with trichotomous Time. But now we cannot even see the past simple as in direct oppostion to the present simple, if we see that form as only one manifestation of the basic form. The question which naturally arises is *What are the defining characteristics* of *the form traditionally thought of as the past simple?* Because there is a dichotomous choice between the first form (present simple) and the second form (past simple) of the verb, it is only when we have understood the *difference* between the two, that the particular characteristics of either will be completely clear. We turn, therefore, in the next Chapter to the defining characteristics of the second form. Those characteristics, in combination with the description in this Chapter, represent one of the primary distinctions of meaning possible within the English verb.

9. The Second Form of the Verb

English possesses only two tense forms. We have seen that we may deal with all of the first as uses of the basic form. We expect the "past simple" to share certain features with the "present simple", and to have certain features which contrast with it.

We have already noted that the "past simple" cannot be uniquely associated with Past Time; some uses of the form refer to Present Time or Future Time:

What name was it please?
I'd tell you if I knew.

Similarly, it is possible to talk about Past Time without using this form of the verb: *I've already seen him.*

Clearly it is not possible to identify the past simple uniquely with Past Time. The Principle of General Use means we must look for a wider underlying meaning. The essential shared characteristic of the basic form and the second form, is that in each case the form is used to describe what the speaker sees as facts, rather than, for example, speculations or psychological interpretations.

We have already met the form traditionally called the "graphic present". It is relatively common in the spoken language and provides us with a route to understanding the contrast between the two English tense forms:

I was sitting there talking to Mark when Dick walked in. He looked furious... then suddenly, up he comes shouting at me, picks up my drink and throws it all over me. I had no idea what was going on.

The traditional name gives us a clear idea of why the form is used — the speaker makes the story more graphic, more immediate to the listeners, by changing from "the past" to "the present". Clearly the speaker could have said: *Up he came, picked up my drink . . .* The referential meaning is the same but the immediacy is lost.

Look at this the other way round — if the shift to the basic form makes the narrative more immediate, the "past" form is less immediate, or more *remote* than the basic form. This contrast is one of the most fundamental in the English verb. The choice between the two traditional tense forms expresses the contrast, from the speaker's point of view, between *immediate* and *remote* events or actions. Although these descriptions provide a key to understanding the contrast, they are not, as yet, an explanation of the use of the forms. We need to enquire more carefully into what is meant by "remoteness".

The past simple for Past Time

Perhaps surprisingly, the idea of remoteness is even helpful in looking at the most straightforward uses of the second form. Many uses of this form, of course, refer to Past Time and are what most people would think of as obvious uses of the past tense:

I saw him yesterday.
I knew her years ago. We were at school together.

The second form is used if the speaker sees the action as remote in time. This may seem obvious, but two important points need to be made:

a. This form is only appropriate for remote facts. *Next week* is in reality as far from Now as *last week* but, while the objective factuality of the past makes *I met her last week* possible, the speculative, non-factual, quality of the future means that **I met her next week* is not possible.

b. We have already noted that it is possible to talk about Past Time without using the "past tense". In many situations there is more than one well-formed way of giving the same referential meaning. The choice depends upon the speaker's interpretation of the situation. Both of the following are correct:

Did you see Jack this morning?
Have you seen Jack this morning?

Both may refer to the same event which is in Past Time. The use of forms containing *(have)* + *third form* is discussed in the next chapter. We see immediately, however, that the second example is more immediate. The speaker will choose *Did you ...?* if, at the moment of speaking, (s)he sees the event as remote. In this particular example, *Have you seen ...?* is usually preferred when the prospect of meeting still remains. This interpretation, however, is derived from the primary semantic distinction. The fact that *Have you seen ...?* is immediate, means that, with particular examples, interpretations such as "still being possible" will be natural. As always, it is important to remember that the interpretation of particular examples in context derives from a combination of factors including expectation, and the primary semantic distinction. In the case of the past simple, the primary semantic characteristic is remoteness.

The concept of remoteness is helpful with a number of other examples, traditionally dealt with in a variety of different ways:

(1) What name was it please?
   Did you want to speak to me immediately?

These forms are appropriate to more formal situations. The first, for example, might be used by a hotel receptionist to a guest. Such uses would be inappropriate in cases where the two speakers had a close relationship. They are appropriate when the relationship between the speakers is relatively remote, in a relatively formal business-like situation. The primary semantic characteristic of the second form explains this use in the same way that it explains other "past tense" uses.

(2) I'd tell you if I knew.

Conditional sentences of the following types:
(a) *I'll ask him if I see him.*
(b) *I'd ask him if I saw him.*

are frequently referred to as *likely* and *unlikely* conditions. In case (a) there is a fairly strong possibility that I will see him; in case (b) there is a *relatively remote* possibility of us meeting. The primary semantic distinction again provides an explanation.

(3) If you know . . . I'm sure you'll tell me.
 If you knew . . . what I've been through, you wouldn't laugh.

Sometimes, Teaching Grammars discuss sentences containing conditions as if they were quite different from simple sentences. This may be helpful for teaching the *forms* of the verb which are used in particular sentences, but it is not a helpful approach to understanding the *meaning* of the verb forms. The meaning of the verb form in any verb phrase, in a simple sentence or in a clause in a complex sentence, is always made up in the same way. In example (2) we saw two possible well-formed sentences with similar meanings. Here we see that the choice of the immediate or remote form immediately after *If,* raises quite different expectations of how the sentence will end.

If you know. . . suggests a real possibility in the forefront of the speaker's mind (immediate to the speaker). *If you knew. . .* automatically suggests *but you don't.* The fact of your knowing is remote from the speaker. The primary semantic distinction provides a satisfactory explanation again.

(4) He said he knew.
 She said it was raining.

Many readers will be familiar with the terms *direct speech* and *indirect speech.* The former consists of the exact words used by the speaker, while in the latter the speaker's words are reported, after verbs such as *say, tell, ask* etc.

Some books have devoted long sections to explaining and practising "rules" for converting direct speech into indirect speech. Swan observes that such "rules" are unnecessary, and that it is sufficient to choose the verb form "naturally" (see *Practical English Usage,* paragraphs 534,5).

Sometimes, non-native teachers who were brought up on the old "rules" trust the rules more than natural language use. This is a mistake. All of the following are completely natural:

He said he knows.   She said it's raining.   He wanted to know if we're going.
He said he knew.   She said it was raining. He wanted to know if we were going.

In each case the speaker has a free choice between the two sentences in each pair.

If, at the moment of speaking, the idea uppermost in the speaker's mind is the words of the speaker which are being reported, it is more than likely that the basic, immediate form of the verb will be chosen.

If the speaker's attention at the moment of speaking is more on *said* or *asked,* in other words if the original words are more remote from the speaker, at the time of speaking, not surprisingly the second, remote verb form is appropriate.

It is important to grasp that it is not a question of one being "right", and one "wrong". Nor is it a matter that one is more or less formal, or more or less "suitable" for the written language. It *is* true, however, that written reports will tend to be more remote, and therefore the remote form will be more frequent. In spontaneous speech, the speaker has a free choice of two equally correct forms, and both occur frequently.

Swan is right — reported speech is not the special case it is sometimes made out to be. In fact, three possibilities exist:

He says he's going to buy one.
He said he's going to buy one.
He said he was going to buy one.

The fourth sentence:

He says he was going to buy one.

also exists, though with a different meaning which is discussed in Chapter 12.

The old-fashioned "rules" of reported speech were invented by teachers and writers to explain away something which causes no difficulty providing we take the Principle of General Use seriously, and keep in mind the primary semantic characteristics of a form. *Remoteness* is a full and systematic explanation of the choice of verb forms appropriate after "reporting verbs".

(5) I would imagine he knew by now.

This contrasts with sentences like:

He knows.
I suppose he knows by now.
I imagine he knows by now.
I would imagine he knows by now.

The speaker gradually distances himself from the factual observation *He knows* by a variety of grammatical choices. Example (5) suggests a situation such as a politician being interviewed or a witness being cross-examined in court. In both cases the speaker is protecting himself from the possibility that his supposition may be incorrect. For some reason he wishes to *distance himself* from the plain factual statement. The addition of *would* (see Chapter 14) and the use of *knew* are distancing elements. They make the statement *more remote* from the speaker.

Contrasting Examples

We have just looked at a group of sentences, each expressing the same referential meaning. It is easier to understand the contribution to the total meaning of any individual element of the verb form if we examine groups such as this. In referring to an event in Past Time, three sentences are suggested:

I came here a lot as a child.
I used to come here a lot as a child.
I would come here a lot as a child.

These are "alternatives" only in the sense that they have the same referential meaning — they give the same factual information. In addition to giving the same factual information, however, the choice of verb form indicates the speaker's perception of, or attitude towards, the event.

The example with *would* is discussed more fully in Chapter 14. Here, we may observe that the "past simple" is used to give information which the speaker sees as *factual*, and *remote*, in this case remote in time. We may say the speaker describes the bare facts.

Would is a modal auxiliary and, like the other modal auxiliaries, introduces a non-factual element into the speaker's interpretation. If the past simple is factually remote, we may perhaps call *would* psychologically remote. It is for this reason that examples such as *I would come. . .* frequently have a feeling of nostalgia or longing — they are associated with the speaker's psychological perception of the earlier time.

Allsop describes this use of *would (Cassell's Student Grammar of English*, as "an alternative in narrative" to *used to*. This suggests there is no intrinsic difference, and that the choice is arbitrary. This is not so. *Would* always introduces an element of psychological remoteness into what the speaker is saying. In different contexts the communicative implications of this psychological remoteness are different, but *would*, like the other modal auxiliaries, is used consistently. It contributes meaning systematically to compound verb forms.

Used to

English possesses a form used specifically for Past Time: *I used to come here when I was a child.*

It is frequently thought that the defining characteristics of this form are:

(i) The situation referred to *was* true in the past.
(ii) It is *not* true at the moment of speaking.

This is true of *almost* all examples of the use of the form: with *He used to live in Scotland*, it *is* possible that he lives in Scotland at the moment of speaking; the defining characteristics are:

(i) The statement *was true* for a *period* in the past.
(ii) For a period subsequent to that during which the statement was true, the statement was *not* true.

In most cases this second period will include the point Now, but this is not necessarily the case. It is, for example, possible for an elderly person who has just moved back to the town of their childhood to say: *It's so nice to be back. I used to live here when I was a child, you know.*

The form differs from the remote form in that examples of *used to* refer to two times — that during which the statement was true, and that during which is was *not*.

The "past tense" modal auxiliaries

The modal auxiliaries are discussed in detail in Chapters 13 and 14. Traditionally, however, some modal auxiliaries are thought of as "the past tense" of others:

Can	**Could**
Will	**Would**
Shall	**Should**

We shall see in Chapter 14 that, rather than regarding them as "the past tense", once again the concept of *remoteness* is useful.

Perhaps *I could speak better French when I was at school* refers to Past Time, but clearly:

I could come tomorrow.
Could you pass the salt please?

are in no sense past forms of the corresponding:

I can come tomorrow.
Can you pass the salt please?

The connection between the pairs, however, becomes clear if the concept of remoteness is introduced. *I can come. . .* means *it is possible for me to come;* the corresponding sentence with *could* means *it is more remotely possible . . . Could,* rather than *can,* is appropriate in "polite requests", that is to say, in situations in which the relationship between the two speakers is more remote; it parallels other uses of the second form to express remote relationships.

In the classroom

Of course it remains likely that teachers will introduce students to the Past Time use of the second form before introducing the concept of remoteness. I am certainly not suggesting that this strategy is in any way unsound. It is, however, helpful, as so-called "other uses" are introduced, to show that they do have something in common with the use students are already familiar with. Teachers often emphasise differences and irregularity; it is helpful to draw attention also to similarities where these exist. This gives a view of the language as a coherent system consistently used by its native speakers. If the concept of remoteness is introduced at an appropriate time in the teaching programme, time will be saved and confusion reduced as students build up an understanding of a primary semantic distinction of English.

Summary

There is an underlying similarity of meaning of *all* uses of what is traditionally called "the past simple". The similarity is that in all cases the speaker conceptualises the action as *factual* but with an element of *remoteness*. The remoteness may be of different kinds — remoteness in time (the most common), remoteness of relationship, possiblity, etc. The traditional "indirect speech" uses are also remote.

10. The Third Form of the Verb with (have).

We look now at verb forms made with the auxiliary *(have)*. Traditionally they are called perfect forms. Technically these are not tenses, but aspects in English. It is characteristic of an aspect that the meaning of the form is specifically associated with the speaker's temporal interpretation of the event. Here are some examples of the form:

I've known him for years.
I've never met them before.
Don't worry, I'll have seen him before Saturday.
You must have wondered what on earth was going on.
It's been specially written for children.
I've been going to tell you for ages.

Each verb form contains part of the verb *(have)* — has, have, had — and the form of the verb known traditionally as the past participle.

The term *past participle* is particularly confusing since it is used for the so-called *present* perfect, *I've just seen him.* This form of the verb is used with *(have)* to make "perfect" forms and with *(be)* to make passive forms. It is always part of a compound verb. The term past participle seems unnecessarily confusing, and, since the form only occurs as part of a compound verb phrase, there is some advantange to using the term *compound form.* It is also true, however, that when students learn the forms of irregular verbs from a table:

bring - brought - brought
go - went - gone

this form is listed as *the third form,* and it is this simple term which is adopted throughout the rest of this book.

It is comparatively easy to see the essential characteristic of the meaning of the form if we consider these examples:

I've met him before. (i.e. *before* Now)
I'd met him before. (i.e. *before* the meeting I just mentioned)
I'll have seen him before I see you. (i.e. *before* a specified future point)

these examples clearly suggest that *(have)* + *third form* is associated with "beforeness".

We have already noted that the two tense forms are used when the speaker is giving a simple factual statement of the situation. "Perfect" forms provide a temporal interpretation. *A University Grammar of English,* gives the significance of this form in a single brief phrase: *The choice of perfective aspect is associated with time orientation.* We have here an idea which we have not discussed earlier in this book. In Chapter 6 we explored different possibilities which might be expressed in the verb form — the difference between points and periods, or complete or uncompleted actions. Here we meet a new idea — the idea of *direction* or orientation in time.

Past Time is, of course, time before the point Now. English verb forms, however, make an important difference between "past" time, and "before Now" time. The first, expressed through the use of the second form, expresses a fact remote in time. It is, so to speak, a "pure" past. Forms made with *(have)* + *third form* look at the past *from the point Now*. These forms look *back* in time. The best descriptive name for them is probably *retrospective* forms. This term is adopted through the rest of this book.

We may say that the remote form expresses the pure facts, without relation to any other point in time, *I saw him*. The present retrospective, *I've seen him*, talks about Past Time looked at from the point Now.

The most important thing to understand about "the present perfect", or present retrospective, is that it is a present form. It is always essentially grounded at the point Now, the moment of speaking.

There is some parallel between the contrast of past simple and present perfect, and the contrast between, *Joan is 34.   Joan is younger than me.*

The first is a simple factual statement; the second is a less specific statement but *relative* to another point. *Joan is younger than me* has direction in a way which is similar to *I've already met him*. *A University Grammar of English*, paragraph 3.31, has this to say:

> Through its ability to involve a span of time from earliest memory to the present, the perfective has an indefiniteness which makes it an appropriate verbal expression for introducing a topic of discourse. As the topic is narrowed down, the emerging definiteness is marked by the simple past. . .

This is a concise statement of the idea that "past" is not the same as "before Now". The "before Now" quality of the retrospective form means it is frequently appropriate for general questions. This is clear if we contrast the pair:

Did you visit the Tower of London?
Have you visited the Tower of London?

The first refers to a single event seen by the speaker as in some way remote — in this case remote in time. The second suggests *Have you ever visited the Tower of London (before Now)?* It relates to the speaker's perception of the action from Present Time, the point Now. From Now the speaker is *looking back*.

It is even easier to see the significance in the case of the past retrospective:

Q *Was David there yesterday?*
A *Yes, but I'd already had a chance to ask him the previous evening.*

The *already* again shows that the speaker is *looking back*, on this occasion from a point in Past Time rather than the point Now.

The form also exists in some combinations which are at first sight surprising:

Oh, don't worry. I'll have seen him before Saturday.

In this case the speaker is looking back from a point in Future Time. (Traditionally this would be called "the past in the future"). The primary semantic characteristic of *(have)* + *third form* forms remains the same, the speaker is looking back.

> *I've been going to ring you for ages.*

In this example the speaker again looks back on the action described by *going to ring*. The use of this form is discussed in the next chapter but, as we shall see there, the meaning of the total form is a combination of the meanings of the *(have)* + *third form* and *(be) going to* factors.

Limited Retrospection

The present restrospective looks back from the point Now. There may be no restriction on the period over which the speaker looks back, *Men have never lived free from fear of war.* The period may be restricted by the real world, *I've never been to America.* Or the speaker may introduce a specific temporal restriction: *I haven't seen him for 3 months/since I last met you.*

The restriction may be given by expressing the period with *for*, or by giving the point at the beginning of the period with *since*. Contextually, of course, other restrictions may apply, *Have you been to the Doctor yet?*, which may apply to the period between us last discussing your illness and Now. In every case the speaker looks back from the point Now to the past.

The past simple and the present perfect

The difference between the use of the remote and the present retrospective forms causes great difficulty for many learners. Particular difficulties arise for many European learners as the distinctions made by the verbal systems of their own language, while in some ways structurally similar to those of English, are semantically very different. The distinction, as we have seen, is that the past simple is essentially factual, remote (in time), and relates to a definite event or state in the past; the present retrospective, is, most importantly a present form, essentially grounded in the moment of speaking. It is also indefinite, and provides the speaker's present view of the past. This explanation, however, is unlikely to help students meeting the forms for the first time in the classroom. This is one of those fundamental distinctions of English which students will take a long time to understand. Teachers must be patient, unafraid of contrasting "difficult" examples, and not expect too much too soon.

Some mistaken ideas

"The recent past"

Teachers should be warned against giving certain common, but misleading explanations. A speaker is more likely to look back on recent events than those further away in time. This has led some teachers and textbook writers to suggest that such forms refer to the *recent* past. While this is *frequently* true, such a statement contradicts our Principle of General Use, and creates such "exceptions" as:

There have been important geological changes in the last two million years.
Have you ever been to France?

Both of these may refer to *comparatively* recent events, or events which occurred a *comparatively* long time ago. It is not helpful to introduce the idea of the "recent" past into classroom explanations of this form.

"Relevance"

A similar difficulty arises with the explanation of the form as "the past tense with present relevance". Clearly a speaker would not look back on an event which was irrelevant to him! It does not, however, help to introduce the idea of "relevance" with examples like: *Who's been sitting in my chair?*

"Relevance" is a difficult idea and does not identify the primary semantic distinction associated with *(have)* + *third form* forms. It is better to use the explanation based on the essential meaning of the form — "the speaker sees, or thinks of, something at the moment of speaking which makes him *look back* on something which has already happened." In this example the cushions on my chair are disturbed, and I notice the *present* effect. This makes me think about something that happened earlier, so, looking back from Now, I say *Who's been sitting in my chair?*

Sometimes the language the speaker uses is almost sufficient to guarantee the use of the present perfect, *Oh look, someone's opened the window.* The use of *Oh look,* places the speaker psychologically very firmly at Now. In these circumstances it is *almost* certain that the speaker will use a present retrospective. At the same time it is not inevitable. The speaker may, thinking almost immediately of an earlier discussion about the windows, say *Oh look, someone opened the window after all.* All we can say is that if the context is such that the speaker is strongly aware of the moment of speaking, Now, present retrospective forms are common.

It is not always the case that the situation referred to is still true, although this is normally the case.

A Which is the nearest tube station to the National Gallery?
B Let's ask John, he's lived in London.

This may be said whether John lives in London now or not, although it is more likely that he does *not* now live in London. In contrast, *He lived in London* necessarily suggests the period of residence referred to definitely finished at a point in the past.

Once again contrasting sentences with similar referential meaning is helpful:

I used to study French.
I studied French.
I've studied French.

The first sentence carries the extra meaning *but I don't any more;* the second is a simple statement of fact *I studied French; what did you do?* while the third suggests a situation such as *so I can translate that letter you have in your hand (now).*

The past retrospective

The past retrospective is similar in every way to the present retrospective except that instead of the events being before Now, they are before a particular point in Past Time:

I hadn't heard. (until you told me)
We'd met before. (i.e. *before* yesterday's meeting)

Somebody had taken my car. (*before* I went to pick it up from the car park)

Complex forms

(have) + *third form* is often a factor in more complicated verb forms:

We'll definitely have got some new stock in before Saturday.
They must have had to wait.
You could have told me!

Summary

In every case the form made with *(have)* + *third form* contributes in the same way to the meaning of the verb form. Its fundamental meaning is that the speaker is looking back. The abstract explanation of retrospection provides a framework within which all other classroom hints can be understood.

"Have I told you about the operation I should have had?"

11. Forms with (be) going to

In the last chapter we saw that English has verb forms used to express retrospection. It immediately seems natural to ask whether corresponding *prospective* forms exist, used when the speaker is *looking forward*. Such forms do exist although they have not usually been identified as such. They are characterised formally by the use of *(be) going to:*

Are you going to tell him?
Don't worry, I was going to tell you anyway.
We were going to meet last Saturday but she was ill.
I'm glad you asked me — I've been going to tell you for ages.
They must be going to widen the road.
I'll be going to see him as soon as he comes out of hospital.

We may begin by considering examples in the present:

(1) *It's going to rain.*
(2) *I think I'm going to sneeze.*
(3) *What are you going to do about it?*

Clearly all such forms are 'present', but relate to Future Time. It is relatively easy to understand the use of *(be) going to* by considering the analogy with forms made with *(have)* + *3rd form.* The speaker uses a *(be) going to* form if (s)he is looking forward. In the case of the present *(be) going to* forms, this means looking forward from the point Now to the future event.

The question immediately arises as to *why* the speaker looks forward from Now to a future event. Something at the moment of speaking must cause the speaker to look forward. We might expect that there would be *evidence* at the moment of speaking for the event referred to by the speaker. The three examples above allow us to see this idea more clearly. In sentence (1) there is evidence — the gathering black clouds — which is available both to the speaker and others. In sentence (2) there is still concrete evidence — the tickle in the nose — but, on this occasion, it is available only to the speaker. Both examples are associated, however, with the existence of evidence. It is absurd when someone says *I think I'm going to sneeze* to ask *What makes you say that?* — we know the speaker has a reason, a concrete reason based on immediate evidence, for what (s)he says.

It may appear that sentence (3) is different but, providing we extend the concept of evidence to include *internal* evidence, knowledge the speaker has at the moment of speaking, when basing a statement on a plan or decision, these examples, too, are seen to be similar.

In general, prospective forms with *(be) going to* are associated with evidence at the moment of speaking. This evidence does not occur instantaneously at the moment of speaking; it is cumulative. The future event is seen as the natural outcome of other events leading up to the point Now. It may be paraphrased as *given the sequence of events up to and including Now, the future event is a natural consequence.*

As we shall see in Chapter 17, when we contrast the different verb forms available in English to talk about Future Time, the differences between the different forms are sometimes small. Even so, it will be characteristic of those forms containing *(be) going to,* that there is *evidence,* leading up to and at the moment of speaking, for the future event.

A practical classroom problem

When students first meet this form it is important to ensure that they do not confuse:

I'm going to the theatre and *I'm going to ask him.*

The first contains the present continuous of the main verb **(go)**. In the second example, *(be) going to* is used as an auxiliary with the main verb **(ask).**

When students first meet *(be) going to* forms, it can help them with the problem of identification if they are given sorting practices (see page 165) such as the following:

> Divide these examples into two groups:
>   a. Those with *go* used as a full verb.
>   b. Those with *(be) going to* used as auxiliary.
>
> 1. Where are you going?
> 2. What are we going to do about it?
> 3. Where are you going for your holidays?
> 4. Are you going to the match on Saturday?
> 5. Are you going to go on Saturday?
> 6. That's enough! I'm not going to tell you again!
> 7. I'm not going to go if it costs as much as that.

It is important that students can identify examples before trying to understand the primary semantic characteristics of the *(be) going to* forms.

Some readers will have met the "explanation" that *(be) going to* forms are "short for" *going to go.* There is no justification for this explanation. It is possible to say both of *Are you going on Saturday?* and *Are you going to go on Saturday?* with slightly different meanings.

The speaker has a free choice and, as we have discussed already, a difference in form implies a difference of meaning. The explanation that one form is "short for" another, is unjustifiable and unhelpful. It confuses, and most importantly, distorts a regular feature of the structure of the English verb.

Other prospective forms

It is now comparatively easy to see the same feature in uses of the past prospective:

I was going to speak to him yesterday, but I'm afraid I missed him.
Now, what was I going to ask you?

"While you were getting ready, I
went to see the film we were
going to see."

In each case the speaker was looking forward at an earlier point in time because of evidence or a plan available at that time.

In Chapter 6 we discussed the kinds of temporal distinction which might be possible within the verb. We now have two forms which we did not foresee at that time, retrospective and prospective. Each is associated with the orientation or direction in time of the speaker's view.

We may also note that past prospective forms may relate to events intended to occur in reality either in Past Time, or in Future Time.

I was going to tell you, but I didn't see you yesterday. (real Past Time)
I was going to tell you tomorrow, after the meeting. (real Future Time)

It is usually thought that if this form is used the event has not taken place. This is not strictly true; what *is* true, is that the plan the speaker had was not realised. The event itself may have occurred *(I told you)*, but not in the planned manner (not at the time and place of my choosing). It is examples such as these that remind us strongly that the speaker's choice of verb form is not only based on the expression of referential meaning, objective fact. Equally important to the choice of verb is the speaker's understanding or perception of the event described. The importance of this in turn is that *any* attempt to describe certain grammatical choices objectively is doomed to failure. Account needs to be taken of the centrality of the speaker.

(be) going to in complex forms

The following example is quite natural:

I've been going to give you a ring for a couple of days.

The example contains both retrospective and prospective forms. Although quite complicated, it is easy to see how each structural feature contributes to the total meaning. The speaker looks *back,* using *(have)* + *third form,* on the prospective, planned, action expressed through the use of *(be) going to.*

Such "complicated" natural examples are reassuring. If they can be analysed in exactly the same way as simpler examples, the general validity of the primary semantic characteristics is supported.

It is also possible to say:

I'll be going to see him as soon as he comes out of hospital.

Here we see two different references to Future Time, one marked by *'ll,* the other by *(be) going to.* The expression is possible, but, as we might expect from the idea of "the future in the future", is comparatively unusual. It is discussed on page 119.

We noted earlier that sometimes the order of elements in a complex verb form is important. If it is possible to "look back on looking forward" *(I've been going to . . .),* is it also possible to "look forward on looking back"? Is the form **I'm going to have seen him* possible?

Some speakers would consider the form permissible, but there is little doubt that *I'll have seen him* is more likely. This, too, is reassuring — it is possible but unlikely that I will have evidence now for having seen him at some time in the future. It is much more likely, as we shall see when we examine the meaning of *will/'ll* in Chapters 13 and 14, that a combination of *will* and *(have) + third form* factors will be appropriate and that, correspondingly, *I'll have seen him* is more likely to occur.

Summary

English has a set of verb forms in which the speaker looks *forward* in time. The forms are characterised structurally by *(be) going to.* These forms, which do not have a traditional name, can be referred to as *prospective* forms. They are used when the speaker has evidence — either external, or internal (in the form of a plan or decision), which provides a reason for looking forward in time.

12. Forms with (be) + . . . ing

So far we have looked at the two English tense forms, and aspects which allow the speaker to look back or forward in time. In every case, however, further temporal interpretation may be given by the speaker by using a form containing *(be)* + . . . *ing*. In theory *(be)* + . . . *ing* may be added to any form of a main verb ("in theory" because the primary semantic characteristics of *(be)* + . . . *ing* forms sometimes conflict with the semantics of a particular verb so that, although this form is in theory possible — it would be a well-formed English sentence — the internal semantic conflict means the form does not, in fact, occur). The forms are usually called *continuous* or *progressive*. They occur in combination with other tense and aspect forms:

(1) It's raining.
(2) He was waiting for me.
(3) He was just leaving as I arrived.
(4) I've been waiting since Christmas.
(5) I'll be seeing him tomorrow.
(6) I think they must be trying to annoy you.
(7) The new hospital is being opened tomorrow.
(8) I listened to the tape while it was being edited.

From a range of examples such as this we see that this form is a "factor" which may be combined with others to create total meaning. As usual, our objective is to identify the primary semantic characteristics which relate to *all* uses of *(be)* + . . . *ing* forms.

We need to remember that this form is not technically a tense, but an aspect. Aspects give the speaker's temporal interpretation of the event. They do not refer to *real* time, but to psychological time — to the *speaker's* perception of the temporal quality of the event.

We need also to remember that we are searching for the primary semantic characteristics of *(be)* + . . . *ing* forms. The communicative or contextual meaning of any sentence is a combination of expectation, situation, and the basic meanings of the words and structures used. We need to think for a moment of the last two elements mentioned — the basic meanings of the *words,* and *structures.* As we seek the basic meaning of *(be)* + . . . *ing* forms, we will see that the intrinsic meaning of certain lexical verbs means they are incompatible with the primary semantic characteristics of *(be)* + . . . *ing* forms. Verbs with such meanings "do not occur in the continuous form" (but see below). Some verbs have meanings which make the use of *(be)* + . . .*ing* either obligatory, or at least very frequent. Some verbs have more than one basic lexical use, sometimes two or more closely related semantic uses, in which *(be)* + . . .*ing* will be obligatory or frequent with one sense, while impossible or unusual with another. In summary, the speaker can interpret temporal features of reality, but not produce internally inconsistent verb phrases.

The best way to search for the primary semantic characteristics of *(be)* + . . .*ing* forms is to examine a number of contrasting pairs, in each of which one verb phrase contains the *(be)* + . . .*ing* factor while the other does not.

The present continuous — longer than a moment

Certain verbs, in which the saying of the sentence *is* the meaning of the sentence, occur in the basic form — the present simple — to refer to the point Now:

I propose a toast.
I pronounce you man and wife.
I swear by almighty God to tell the truth. . .

In these sentences it would be inappropriate to say **I am proposing, *I am pronouncing,* or **I am swearing.*

With these declarative verbs, the saying of the sentence is the action referred to. Clearly it takes a defininte period of time to say *I propose a toast.* In real time the action occurs for a period. In psychological time, however, the speaker treats this period as if it were a single point in time, the point Now. We have already seen that the basic form is appropriate to events coincident with the point Now.

The situation may be unusual, but it is not impossible to imagine someone bursting into a group of people sitting around a table exclaiming *What on earth are you doing?* to which one of the others present replies *I'm proposing a toast.* This sentence, although extremely unusual, is not impossible. Now, however, the speaker has been interrupted while in the act of proposing a toast. No longer is it possible to regard the event, even in psychological time, as a point — points cannot be "interrupted". Clearly, *I am proposing* relates not to a point, but to a *period.*

In contrast to a verb like *propose,* consider the verb *rain.* The sentence *Oh dear, it's raining,* is common but in the same circumstances it is impossible to say **Oh dear, it rains.* Why?

Experience tells us that it never rains for a single moment but that rain continues for a *period* which surrounds the point Now. With this in mind it is easy to see how the form *It's raining* came to be called the Present Continuous. It is equally easy to see why this form is appropriate to answer the question *What are you doing?* and how teachers and students often associate it with "an action going on at the time of speaking". It is very often introduced into English lessons by teachers acting and using the question and answer pair:

Q What am I doing?
A You're reading/writing/playing the piano/waving.

So far, we see that this form is not appropriate for events which the speaker conceptualises as occurring at a single point, while it is appropriate for actions which cover a *period* of time. This is not, however, the whole story. We need to contrast:

I live in Oxford.   I'm living in Oxford.

The second of this pair is similar to *It's raining,* but what about the first example? It describes an event which is going on at the moment of speaking, which surrounds Now, and which is a period in time. Equally clearly, the event will end at some Future Time — either because I move or, ultimately, because I die. We need to remember, however, that the speaker's choice of verb form both conveys the facts, and his or her attitude to, or interpretation of, those facts. The question is not whether my living in Oxford *is* a period of time but whether, at the moment of speaking on a particular occasion, I wish to emphasise that it is something which will occur for a *limited* period of time.

With *I'm living in Oxford,* the speaker conceptualises a temporary state; in psychological time the period is *limited.* This limit is not suggested by *I live in Oxford.*

The essential characteristic of *(be)* + . . .*ing* forms used for "the present continuous" is that the speaker uses a *(be)* + . . .*ing* form if, at the moment of speaking, (s)he conceptualises the action as existing for a *limited period* of time. Looked at negatively, in psychological time, the action does not occur at a single point (it is not a *punctual* action), nor is it extended for an *unlimited* period.

Although we have now identified the defining characteristics of present *(be)* + . . .*ing* forms, it is useful to look at the same information from a slightly different point of view. The two characteristics of the form are that it describes a *period,* and that that period is *limited.* It is then, of course, true that events described in the present continuous are *incomplete* at the moment of speaking. This is intrinsic to the fact that they extend over a period of time which *includes* the point Now. "Incompleteness" is *not,* however, a complete and satisfactory definition. It omits the essential characteristic that in psychological time the speaker sees the period as limited. We could alternatively say that the speaker sees the action as *incomplete,* but *completable,* already in the process of being completed. Although this way of looking at the event is not particularly helpful for the present continuous, it is of use when considering other continuous forms.

Classroom explanation

The difference between "present simple", and "present continuous" is one of the most frequent sources of misunderstanding for students of English. The basic misunderstanding often stems from a methodology which introduces the present continuous through the teacher's acting (as referred to above). It is perhaps inevitable that teachers will introduce the present continuous in this way. They can, however, at least try to prevent some of the major confusions by bearing in mind that the explanation "an action going on at the moment of speaking" is *not* satisfactory. The explanation of this form requires an understanding of three different ideas:

1. The general point (see Chapter 5) of the difference between grammar as fact and grammar as choice, so that it is not only how long the action took in real time, but the speaker's view of the event.

2. *(be)* + . . .*ing* forms are appropriate if the speaker conceptualises a *period.* This idea *is* conveyed by the idea of "an action going on at the moment of speaking".

3. That the period is *limited*. It is this part of the explanation which is missing from the traditional classroom rule. By drawing attention to this at the appropriate time, as students begin to meet examples like *I live in Oxford*, at least some of the potential confusion can be avoided.

It is not unusual for teachers to 'hide' examples which do not fit the hints which they have given. In fact, as we see throughout this book, it is frequently just those examples which most clearly reveal how the particular structure is used. There is an excellent example:

I usually go to work on the bus but this week I'm taking the car.

A common explanation advanced by teachers is that "The present simple is used for a repeated action, a habit". If that were true, then I would have to say: **But this week I take the car* as, self evidently, the action is repeated throughout the week.

We have already seen that the real explanation is that the *(be) + ... ing* form is appropriate if the speaker sees the action as going on for a *limited* period. This explains both of the examples in this sentence.

Examples such as these, far from being embarrassments that need to be hidden, are the very examples which, if teachers present them carefully, will lead their students to a genuine understanding of how the forms are used, and of the boundaries of meaning between different forms.

Some contrasting pairs

Depending on the meaning of the lexical verb, different situations arise:

1. Each of the pair continuous/non-continuous is possible, though with different meanings:

I play the piano and the guitar.
I'm playing the piano.

The contextual explanation of this pair is the difference between ability, and activity. It is characteristic of activities that the idea of a limited period leads to "an action going on at the moment of speaking". Less obviously, it is the *unlimited* quality of *play* which is the underlying reason for the "ability" interpretation of the first sentence.

2. One form is possible, the other impossible:

I swear I didn't do it.
*I'm swearing I didn't do it.

Declarative verbs, used in their declarative sense, do not take the continuous because they are essentially punctual.

This does not mean, however, the same word cannot occur with a *(be) +* *...ing* form: *What are you swearing about?*
Sometimes what appears similar may be different, so that both of the following are possible:

I tell you I didn't do it.
I'm telling you I didn't do it.

This is because *tell* has two very similar meanings, a declarative one, so *I tell ...* is natural, and a second meaning, *tell* = to describe a situation in words for someone else. In this case *I am telling ...* is natural.

3. Sometimes both are possible with different connotational meanings:

I work in a hospital. — I do not plan to move; it is my permanent job.
I'm working in a hospital. — I expect to move; it is a temporary job.

4. A verb may have two associated meanings, one frequently taking the simple form, the other the continuous;

I think so. (think = believe, which cannot be temporarily restricted.)
Hang on, I'm thinking about it. (think is an activity, and may be limited in the same way as other "activity" verbs.)

Finally, we notice that the limited time quality of the continuous form means it is frequently associated with specific, rather than general, reference:

Where do you go for your holidays? — Usually, general.
Where are you going for your holidays? — This year, specific.

The contrast between general and specific is clearly illustrated by a possible, though slightly unusual use. In referring to any normal word, we could naturally ask *How do you spell. . .?* In asking about *names,* however, it is by no means unusual to be asked *How are you spelling (Lewis)?*

Clearly the question about an ordinary word of the language is a matter of fact, and a verb form reflecting the general nature of the question is appropriate. When a hotel receptionist asks me about my name, however, it is possible for me to spell my name in more than one way. The receptionist asks a specific question.

It is interesting to note that this example is a baffling exception to anyone who believes that "the present continuous is used for an action going on at the moment of speaking". In this case, I am most certainly *not* spelling my name at the moment the question is asked, otherwise the question would be totally redundant! The question could be paraphrased *What spelling of ... is appropriate on this occasion?,* and because of the restrictive nature of the question, a *(be)* + . . .*ing* form is appropriate.

With a few verbs the difference between general and specific becomes so small that for all practical purposes there is no difference of meaning between simple and continuous sentences:

I'm not feeling very well.   *Are you feeling better?*
I don't feel very well.   *Do you feel better?*

As with many grammatical problems, it is possible to provide specific explanations for specific pairs. More interestingly, however, it is also possible to identify primary semantic characteristics for the form. These, as we have seen, cover all uses of the form.

The "past continuous"

If we turn our attention to "past continuous" forms there is little difficulty in seeing that the explanation is still satisfactory. All of the following are possible:

He left when I came in.
He was leaving when I came in.
He left when I was coming in.
He was leaving when I was coming in.

It is also clear that the two actions — *leaving* and *coming in* — will, in general, take approximately the same amount of real time. The concept of grammar as choice, however, means that the speaker has four possibilities and can use these to interpret the temporal relationship between the 'waiting' and the 'coming in'.

We noted earlier that an explanation of these sentences which introduces an idea of causality *(He left because I came in)* is a contextual interpretation, not a general explanation of the use of the form.

The fundamental explanation is that the choice of a remote form means that the speaker conceptualises that action as in Past Time, and the *(be) + . . .ing* form means that the speaker conceptualises that action as existing for a limited period. If, therefore, the speaker sees both events as extended in time, *He was leaving when I was coming in* will be used.

If the speaker sees one action as interrupting another then, necessarily, the interrupted action must be a period and a *(be) + . . .ing* form will be obligatory.

We saw that the speaker uses a remote form, the "past simple", to describe any event which is remote in time but seen as "a pure fact". This raises one of the most difficult points to understand about the English verb. When we looked at the basic form (see page 64) we noted two sentences:

We leave from Paddington.   *We leave at 7.30 tomorrow morning.*

Each sentence refers to a fact. The basic form expresses pure factuality. The second sentence appears to be "the present simple used for the future". This is, however, an illusion. The *We leave* is clearly the same in each of the sentences. The fact that one sentence is about *place* and the second about *time* is an accident. The reason for the choice of verb form in each case is because the speaker conceptualises the event as a fact. That simple explanation is the *whole* explanation of the choice of verb form in those two sentences.

In referring to Past Time, it is of course the remote form of the verb which is appropriate rather than the basic form. In the same way, however, events may be seen as pure facts:

I lived in Grange Road.   *I lived there for 30 years.*

Again, the first sentence is about place, and the second about time but this is incidental to the choice of verb form. In each case the speaker is describing a simple fact, remote in time. The difficulty is that the second sentence is clearly about a period, and indeed about a limited period, in real time. We might, therefore, expect a "past continuous" form. Despite the explicit time reference, *for 30 years,* in psychological time, the speaker will see this simply as a single entity in Past Time, without temporal interpretation. In particular, although the speaker refers explicitly to the period, it is not necessary to conceptualise the event as a period within the verb form.

Readers are reminded that it is possible to say *in London* or *at London.* The second does not mean that the speaker has lost sight of the size of London, only that the speaker wishes to refer to London as a precise point, so that "at-ness", rather than "in-ness" is appropriate. In the same way *I lived there for 30 years* does not mean the speaker has forgotten that 30 years is a period, only that no attention is drawn to this in the verb form.

The parallel is even closer than might appear at first. The preposition *in* will be appropriate with London if the speaker, for any reason, needs London to be an extended space. Part of the concept of "in-ness" is extension in space. Things which happen "in", are enclosed or bounded by the place they happen "in". Verb forms with *(be) +...ing* are similar. By their use, the speaker draws particular attention to the fact that a period, extended in time, is involved. Other events can then occur within the period, bounded by the limits of the period.

It is essential to remember that the verb form is not decided by the objective question of whether or not a period in real time was involved. A *(be) +...ing* verb form is appropriate if, and only if, the speaker wishes to draw *particular* attention to the fact that a "space in time" is involved. For an interrupted action, a *(be) +...ing* form will be obligatory, since the concept of interruption necessarily implies extension in time. In many cases however, it is possible to describe an event in Past Time with either the remote form or "the past continuous", depending entirely on the speaker's interpretation of the event.

Not "the longer of two actions"

It is not the *real* time taken by an action which is important, but the speaker's perception of the action. Consider the following diagram:

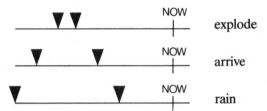

The lines indicate the real time, the actual duration, of each event. But the following examples are both correct:

It was raining when the Queen arrived.
The bomb exploded while the Queen was arriving.

The Queen's arrival took the same time in each case. The speaker's perception of the actions, however, differs and the speaker needs the *(be) +...ing* form for the longer action. This is typical of such forms used with Past Time reference. It is *not* however true that the form is used *because* one action is longer than the other. It is because of the speaker's perception. If the speaker sees one action as "contained within" another, the containing action *must* be interpreted as extended in time, and a *(be) +...ing* form becomes obligatory.

In the classroom teachers frequently use the idea of one action being longer than another to discuss these two forms. Most readers will have met the sentence *She was having a bath when the telephone rang.* The explanation offered is invariably that the shorter action is in the "past simple", while the longer is in the "past continuous". Such an explanation totally overlooks the fact that it is not the real time taken. While it "explains away" that particular example, which has been chosen to ensure that that explanation fits it, it does not explain that all of the following are possible sentences:

Jack watched television while I did my homework.
Jack was watching television while I was doing my homework.
Jack watched television while I was doing my homework.
Jack was watching television while I did my homework.

The fact that all four are possible can only be explained by reference to the speaker's interpretation of the temporal quality of the event. It is not a matter of what, objectively, "happened".

Interpretation of individual examples can easily confuse. Earlier we considered *He was leaving when I came in*. The verb forms mean the speaker interprets the "leaving" as containing "coming in". It is therefore *possible* that he changed his mind and did not complete his leaving. Such an interpretation depends upon the fundamental semantic charcteristics of *(be)* + ...*ing*. If we consider the example *He left when I came in*, the speaker conceptualises neither action as containing the other. Although the actions are extended in time, the speaker describes them as two remote facts, conceptualised as *points* in time. The hearer may interpret this as two coincident points or, more probably, as two closely consecutive points. In context, this second interpretation can easily lead to causal connection: *He left* because *I came in*. In a particular situation the speaker may even intend this interpretation. The association between cause and effect, however, while an explanation of this particular example, is a consequence of the fundamental semantic charcteristics of the verb forms chosen, not an explanation of them.

While the explanation of "the longer of two actions" is not accurate, it contains a grain of truth. There is an interesting contrast between the "present continuous" and the "past continuous". With many "present" examples, though not all, *(be)* + ...*ing* shortens or "closes down" an event; *I'm living in Oxford,* restricts the generality of *I live in Oxford*. With past time reference, *(be)* + ...*ing* lengthens or "opens out" the action; *I was waiting for you* emphasises the extension in time of the wait in a way that *I waited for you* does not.

This "opening up", or "closing down" is not completely generalisable. *I am suggesting* ... opens up the more common *I suggest* ....

The reason for this *apparent* difference, and it is only an apparent difference, between the use of *(be)* + ...*ing* at different times is that the primary semantic characteristics of forms containing *(be)* + ...*ing* are that the speaker conceptualises the action as occurring between precisely two points in time — the action is *longer* than an instant, and *shorter* than an unlimited period. In any particular use of a *(be)* + ...*ing* form, the emphasis may be on either of these factors. On the whole, though not always, the emphasis with "present continuous" is on the *limited* nature of the period, while with Past Time reference, the emphasis is usually on the *extension* in time.

The University Grammar of English observes (paragraph 3.33):

> As with the present, the progressive when used with the past specifies the limited duration of an action. ...
>
> In consequence, it is a convenient device to indicate a time span within which another event (indicated by the simple past) can be seen as taking place. ...
>
> The ability to express incomplete action with the progressive is illustrated strikingly by: *The girl was drowning in the lake* (will permit "but someone dived in and rescued her")
> *The girl drowned in the lake.*

It will be noted that they look first at the primary semantic charcteristics, to show how these will permit interpretations in particular contexts. This approach, emphasised throughout the present book, contrasts strongly with Thomson and Martinet (page 151) who suggest that:

> The past continuous can be used as an alternative to the simple past to indicate a more casual, less deliberate action:
> *I was talking to Tom the other day.*
> The past continuous here gives the impression that the action was in no way unusual or remarkable. It also tends to remove responsibility from the subject. In the above example it is not clear who started the conversation, and it does not matter. Note the contrast with the simple past tense, *I talked to Tom,* which indicates that I took the initiative.

While much of what they say may be true of the particular example in a certain context, the explanation is *fundamentally* unsound. It is extraordinary to suggest that the verb form is chosen *because* the speaker wishes to indicate "a more casual, less deliberate action". A *(be)* + . . .*ing* verb form is aspectual, and expresses the speaker's interpretation of the temporal nature of the action. Any contextual interpretation results from that interpretation, not the other way round. Many Thomson and Martinet explanations suffer the same defect. They try to describe as if they were matters of objective fact the reasons why the speaker *may* have chosen a particular verb form. Such descriptions can never be more than speculation, and are hardly ever generalisable from example to example. As such they are a potential source of much confusion. Explanations of this kind need to be avoided, both in books and by teachers in the classroom.

Retrospective forms with (be) + . . .ing

One of the main suggestions of this book is that the semantics of a more complicated verb form are simply the semantics of the contributing structural features. If we contrast:

We'd waited 20 minutes before the bus arrived.
We'd been waiting 20 minutes before the bus arrived.

there appears to be a free choice. As we saw with examples contrasting the remote form and the "past continuous", the only difference is the speaker's perception of the action and whether particular attention is drawn to an extension in time through use of a *(be)* + . . .*ing* form.
If we consider:

I've known him for years.
*I've been knowing him for years.

clearly a period of real time is involved *(for years).* But it appears that it is not possible for the speaker to draw particular attention to the extension in time through the verb form. Such problems have frequently been explained away by reference to particular groups of verbs — "verbs like *know* do not occur in the continuous form". Such explanations are unsatisfactory. The statement is meaningless unless we know *in what way* the verbs are "like *know*". If we can answer that question, then we can explain *why* these verbs "do not occur in the continuous form".

Many readers must have found one part of the argument presented so far difficult to accept. When we look at "the past simple", *I lived there for 30 years* presents a problem. It is a period in real time; and it is difficult to imagine the speaker *not* seeing it as a period even in psychological time. So far, the explanation has concentrated on the speaker not wishing to *emphasise* the extension in time. With **I've been knowing him . . .*,this explanation is no longer valid. The speaker has no choice — the continuous form is impossible here. As usual, such initially problematic examples lead us to a deeper understanding of the real semantics.

Traditional terminology talks about the past simple and the present simple; it does not talk about, for example, the present perfect simple. Because there is an aspect involved — perfection — the term "simple" is not applied. Even so, every verb form in English may occur in either the continuous or non-continuous form. In order to understand the significance of the continuous form, we need to understand the significance of non-continuous forms — both those traditionally thought of as "simple" tenses, and those other forms which do not contain *(be) + . . .ing*. In what sense are the simple tenses "simple"? Are other non-continuous forms in some sense "simple" too?

The answer has something to do with why *know* does not occur in the continuous form; something to do with why *I lived there for 30 years* is a possible sentence, despite the apparent conflict between the semantics of the verb and the adverbial phrase. It also has something to do with why *I propose a toast* is a possible form.

A non-continuous form is appropriate if the speaker conceptualises the action as a simple totality; as a single whole. In *at London,* London is conceived of as a single unit; its spacial extent is irrelevant. The speaker concentrates on its unity. Rather than seeing the city as a collection of buildings, spaces, streets etc., it is conceived of as "a place". It's *extension* in space is ignored, as the speaker conceives of it *as a whole.* This is exactly the function of non-continuous verb forms. They express the action as a simple, integrated whole. The action or event is conceived as a unit, in its totality. Extension in time is irrelevant.

It is easy to see the relevance of this explanation to *I propose a toast,* seen as a single immediate act, and *I lived there for 30 years* where the emphasis is on the unitary nature of the event. The speaker regards the act as a *complete* act — notice, not complete *in time,* but complete in an entirely abstract sense.

The problem of **I've been knowing* is solved. In English *knowing* is an indivisible concept, I *know* or I *don't know.* However extended in time my knowing is, it is always conceived of in a single unitary way. For this reason a *(be) + . . .ing* form is not appropriate. The phrase "verbs like *know*" , means states which are, by their very nature, intrinsically unitary or indivisible. (It is not of course true that "knowing" cannot be seen as a process. In this case in English, it is possible to make *I'm getting to know her.* The use of *get to know* expresses the process, the divisibility, of "knowing".)

The more abstract way of regarding the contrast between non-continuous and continuous forms has immediate application to examples such as:

I've learnt some French.
I've been learning some French.

The first conceptualises the learning as a single, unitary whole. Because we are aware of learning as a process which is essentially extended in time, the immediate implication is that I regard my learning as complete. The first sentence clearly suggests that I have now stopped studying French. The second sentence, where the speaker conceptualises the learning as non-unitary, implies that my French studies continue.

It is difficult to find a single word which adequately conveys the essential idea of the non-continuous forms. "Complete" easily suggests "finished", and therefore complete *in time*. While this of course applies to events in Past Time, it does not cover straightforward examples such as *I speak French, I live in Oxford, Water boils at 100 °C*. We may, perhaps, say that with a non-continuous form the speaker sees an event "simply", that is to say without interpreting it. Such a statement is almost circular. The underlying concept is the idea of the "wholeness" of the act or state. Non-continuous forms draw attention to the indivisiblity of what is described, to its *unitary* nature.

We have already noted the tendency of *(be) + . . .ing* forms to "open up" events in Past Time, and "close down" events in Present Time. We now see the reason for this. It is natural to see events in Past Time as whole, complete entities, complete in time. For such events the remote, "past simple" is appropriate. A *(be) + . . .ing* form will only be produced in those cases where the speaker is interested in an event in Past Time, when seen as an incomplete, non-unitary, event.

In contrast, in Present Time most events, of their nature, are not seen as complete wholes. In a few cases, particularly with declarative verbs, such a conceptualisation is natural. Much more frequent, however, will be to describe events which are incomplete in real time, and where the speaker will be interested in the event in progress. In such cases, "progressive", *(be) + . . .ing* forms, will be appropriate.

It is perhaps necessary to repeat that the concept of the action as *complete* refers to an abstraction, not "complete in time". This is of great importance if this explanation is to apply to such uses as *I play the piano,* or *I play tennis every Saturday.* In both cases, the speaker does not see the actions as "events in time", but as complete or unitary in an abstract, non-temporal sense.

The future

Because English has no one verb form uniquely, or even particularly, associated with Future Time the choice of verb form for particular events in Future Time is complex. It is discussed in detail in Chapter 17. We observe here only that the so-called "present continuous as the future", can be shown to have characteristics identical to other uses of "the present continuous". In short, the form is appropriate if the speaker sees two events related — one which pre-dates Now, which causes the speaker to expect the future event, and the future event itself. In *It's raining,* two points surround Now — the start of the rain and the anticipated end of the rain. The speaker describes an event which exists precisely between two points, one on either side of Now. In *I'm playing tennis tomorrow,* the situation is the same. The speaker sees the point before Now — the arrangement which was made — and the point after Now — the game of tennis, so that once again there is an event which, in the speaker's mind, exists *between two points,* one on either side of Now.

Forms with (be) + . . . ing

It is also possible to talk about Future Time using the more complex verb forms:

I'll drive while you sleep.
I'll be lying on the beach while you're working.

In the first example the meaning centres on the semantics of *'ll*. In the second case, the total meaning is a combination of those of *'ll* and *(be) +* *. . .ing*. Notice, however, that in the first example the driving and sleeping are conceptualised as complete wholes, so *(be) + . . .ing* forms are not appropriate. In the second example the speaker conceptualises the lying and working as extended in time, not as complete wholes. For this reason the verb forms contain *(be) + . . .ing*.

The *University Grammar of English* referring to the past progressive, describes it as "a convenient device to indicate a time span within which another event can be seen as taking place". *(be) + . . .ing* forms invariably mean that the event is extended in time. Because of this extension it is possible for that event to "contain" another. For this reason it is sometimes helpful to see *(be) + . . .ing* forms as providing a *background* event. This applies to such uses of *'ll (be) + . . .ing* as *I'll be seeing him tomorrow,* which clearly suggests the surrounding circumstances for an event such as *so I can ask him then.* This "background" idea is also appropriate to examples such as the popular song *She'll be coming round the mountain when she comes.*

The speaker clearly intends *both* events to be seen as extended in time in examples such as:

You will be slaving away at your desk while we're lying on the beach.

"It's all right, dear, I'll be going to bed in a minute."

(be) + always + . . .ing

Expressions containing *(be) + always + . . .ing* are frequently given special treatment in examples such as:

I'm always meeting her at the station.
He's always losing his spectacles.

From a functional point of view such examples express the speaker's surprise or annoyance at the unexpectedly high frequency of the event.

Some books suggest the form is associated with annoyance. Chalker has given an example which clearly shows that this is not the case:

> Contrast *He's always buying me lovely presents* with *He always buys me lovely presents.* I am surely pleased in both cases. But whereas *always + present simple* needs some context for the habit (e.g. for my birthday, whenever he comes to see me) *always + progressive* emphasises the frequent activity itself. The emotional impliction depends on the semantics.

Here Chalker discusses a principle emphasised in this book. A particular example may be interpreted in a particular way, but the primary semantic characteristics of a form are constant. Particular contextual meanings always depend on the fundamental semantics.

In the case of *(be) + always + ...ing* it may be that the implication arises from the conflict of meaning between the open, general meaning of *always, and the temporal restriction of the (be) + ...ing* form. From a classroom point of view it seems clear that this form is best presented lexically without analysis of its constituent parts.

Summary

All forms usually called continuous or progressive contain *(be) + ...ing.* In every case the contribution to the total meaning made by the *(be) + ...ing* element of the verb form is identical. The form is an aspect, so that all forms containing *(be) + ...ing* include an element of the speaker's interpretation of the temporal quality of the event. "Non-continuous" forms express the speaker's view of the event as a complete, unitary whole. In contrast, the "continuous" forms express incompleteness, and, in particular, incompleteness in time. "Incompleteness in time" means that the speaker conceptualises the action as occurring for a *period,* and that that period is *limited.* Forms containing *(be) + ...ing* express the speaker's view of the event as having *limited duration.* For this reason we may conveniently and helpfully refer to them as *durative* forms.

Despite apparent differences, depending upon whether the form is associated with Present Time, Past Time, or a retrospective verb form, the primary semantic characteristics of the form remain constant.

13. The Group of Modal Auxiliaries

We come now to one of the most complicated problems of the English verb. Large books have been written on modality, and even on the more restricted subject of the modal auxiliaries. Palmer, *Modality and the English Modals, Longman 1979,* says of the modals:

> There is no doubt that the overall picture of the modals is extremely "messy" and untidy and that the most the linguist can do is to impose some order, point some regularities, correspondences, parallelisms. . . . This subject is not one that lends itself to any simple explanation.

At the same time, while dismissing the idea of the search for a "basic meaning" which may be attributed to each of the modal auxiliaries, Palmer does suggest that although he does not believe such a basic meaning exists:

> (This) must not be taken to imply that we cannot look for a fairly generalised common meaning or a set of closely related meanings for each modal. It is only when precision is demanded or invariance postulated that the notion of a basic meaning becomes unrealistic.

So, we are warned. The area of the modal auxiliaries is complex, and potentially a minefield. There is, however, a large central area which is systematic and relatively easily understood. Our first task is to identify this central area and, for the moment at least, to remove examples which will obscure the powerful central patterns.

The group of personal pronouns *I, you, he, she, it, one, we, they* — form what is called a closed class of words. Such a closed class consists of a small number of words which:

a. fulfil the same grammatical function

b. are reciprocally defined — *we* means *not I, not you,* etc

c. are reciprocally exclusive — only one such idea may be included in the verb phrase at one time, so that sentences such as **I you live in Castle Street* are impossible, although two may be joined by *and: He and I both went.*

Closed classes represent important areas in the structure of the language. While the language is frequently creating and losing words in open classes (nouns, verbs) it is relatively unusual for a word in a closed class to disappear (although *thou* and *thy* have more or less disappeared from contemporary English) and new members of the closed class do not appear (it is difficult to imagine a new pronoun, or a new preposition). A closed class expresses certain subdivisions to a central, or closely related group of ideas. The modal auxiliaries form such a closed class.

If we list a number of examples the pattern is quickly observed:

(1) *I* **can** *swim.*
(2) *He* **shouldn't** *have done that.*
(3) *They* **must've** *missed the train.*
(4) *He* **might** *not know yet.*
(5) *It* **couldn't** *have been easier.*
(6) *I think she* **may be** *pulling your leg!*

In each of these statements the first place of the verb phrase is occupied by a modal auxiliary. If such an auxiliary occurs in a sentence, it is always the first element of the verb phrase, following the subject in statements. As a closed class they share certain characteristics of meaning and are reciprocally exclusive **I must can ask him* is impossible, although once more two of the closed class may be linked by *and* in the same sentence: *You could and should have checked first.*

The simple observation that the modal auxiliaries occur in the first place in the verb phrase helps us to identify the group of modal auxiliaries. It produces one or two surprises.

Will, shall, 'll in statements such as:

(7) *I will try to let you know.*
(8) *I shall borrow my father's.*
(9) *I'll soon sort this out!*

show that *shall, will,* and *'ll* belong to the modal auxiliary group. They share elements of meaning with the other modal auxiliaries and it is not possible for them to co-occur with the others: **He will can do it.*

The understanding that *shall, will* (and *'ll*) are modal auxiliaries is important. It emphasises that they are not "the future tense". Accurate sorting is a prerequisite of accurate description; the traditional mis-sorting of these items has been a source of much confusion. Recognising them as modal auxiliaries helps clear the way for a deeper understanding of their primary semantic characteristics.

(10) *You may have to press the switch first.*
(11) *They must have had to get a later train.*

(Have) to can co-occur with a modal auxiliary and it does not occur in the first place of the verb phrase. The conclusion we draw is that *(have) to* does not share the characteristics of the group we are seeking. Although closely related in meaning to one of the modal auxiliaries, *must,* there is an important semantic distinction. Learners of English have frequently found the difference between *must* and *(have) to* a source of much confusion. As we shall see below, much of that confusion disappears as soon as we recognise that there is a fundamental difference, and that *(have) to* forms are different in kind from the modal auxiliaries in the basic group.

The complete list

A list of modal auxiliaries may be established by identifying the words which may fill the space in *He . . . come.* The following are undoubtedly possible:

can	shall	may	will	must
could	should	might	would	

Unfortunately, as Palmer has pointed out, the modals are messy. In the above table we note that there appear to be four "pairs", and one odd word, *must.* Is there a reason for this? As we shall see below, the answer is *Yes.*

We have already recognised that *(have) to* should not be included in the list but certain other items may need to be:

He ought to come.   He need not come.   Dare he come?

There is no doubt that *ought to, need* and *dare* appear to share some of the characteristics of the other modal auxiliaries. On the other hand, they appear to be relatively rare and they do not always behave similarly:

Need I ask?   You didn't ought to do that.   Dare we tell him?
Do I need to ask?   You ought not to do that.   Do we dare to tell him?

Clearly there is a full verb *need to,* which semantically has something to do with necessity. (We know it is a full verb because of the third person-**s** in *He needs to be there by 3 o'clock.*) But it appears that there is sometimes an auxiliary *need,* which behaves like a member of the group of modal auxiliaries listed above.

The best way through this confusion is to define as "the modal auxiliaries", the group given above, which *always* behave similarly, and which behave similarly to each other. All of these share a number of important characteristics:

They occupy the first place in a complex verb phrase.
They do not co-occur.
They are used as operators in the formation of, for example, questions, negatives etc. (See chapter 7).
They share important semantic similarities.

For the moment, we will concentrate on this basic group and relegate those auxiliaries which sometimes "misbehave" to the group of *marginal modals.*

What primary semantic characteristics do the modal auxiliaries in the basic group share? With the choice of a pure *tense* form the speaker expresses the factual elements of a situation; with *aspect* the speaker provides an interpretation of the temporal features of an action. Modal auxiliaries allow the speaker to express an attitude to the *non-factual* and *non-temporal* elements of the situation. This means (s)he can introduce elements of possibility, necessity, desirability, morality, doubt, certainty, etc.

Modality in English is realised in a very wide variety of ways:

He's coming.
He's probably coming.
He might come.

The first sentence does not contain a modal expression; the speaker expresses a fact. The second sentence is not factual; it includes an element of modality, introduced by the use of the word *probably.* In this case the modal element of the sentence is not part of the verb. The third example, which is close in meaning to the second, is also non-factual. In this case, modality is introduced through the use of the modal auxiliary *might.*

It is immediately clear that a general discussion of modality — the speaker's interpretation of non-factuality — is an enormous subject. This book is concerned with the English verb. Modal auxiliaries are one element only in the general study of modality. It is also clear that we are moving into a difficult area. We have already seen that the speaker's choice of verb form is frequently much more intensely personal — a matter of choice — than traditional grammar has recognised. This applies to questions of inter-preted or non-interpreted factuality ("the past simple" v "the past continuous"). Now we need to consider choices which reflect the speaker's perception of non-factual comments — speculations, guesses, estimates, idealisations. We must expect that one speaker's perception of such ideas will be very different from another's and that, in consequence, it is unlikely that verbal expressions which realise these ideas will be used completely consistently.

Our explanation needs to follow two steps — What do all of the group of modal auxiliaries *always* have in common? What kind of meaning do they express? When those questions have been solved, we can enquire as to the particular meaning of each member of the group.

The speaker's or listener's judgment

Verb phrases containing a modal auxiliary are different in one important way from those which do not. A verb phrase which does not contain a modal auxiliary is "about" the subject of the sentence. *Peter lives in Grange Road* is "about" Peter. Statements or questions which contain a modal aux-iliary are about *two* people — the subject, and speaker (in statements) or listener (in questions). *Peter may come tomorrow* is about Peter, but also about the speaker's own judgment or opinion.

In the case of a question, the listener's opinion is involved, as well as the person obviously referred to by the sentence. *What should I do?* is clearly about me, but is also equally importantly about the listener's judgment or opinion.

There are three important characteristics of verb phrases containing a modal auxiliary:
1. They are not about facts alone.
2. They are about the speaker's or listener's judgment or opinion at the moment of speaking.
3. They necessarily involve *two* people — the subject and the speaker or lis-tener. If the subject of the sentence is "I" the same person is involved, but in two different ways; *I may come* is a different kind of statement from *I know Carol.*

The modal auxiliaries always express the speaker's (or listener's) judgment or opinion at the moment of speaking. In other words, each modal auxiliary is fundamentally grounded in the moment of speaking, at the point Now. They are "present" forms, not in the traditional sense, but because each may be paraphrased "in the present circumstances, my judgment is that it is possible/necessary/desirable that . . .". This is different from the conventional view that, for example, *could* is "the past tense" of *can*. It is somewhat misleading to regard modal auxiliaries as modal auxiliary *verbs*. In almost no respect do they behave like full verbs (they are used as opera-tors, full verbs are not; they can be used as pro-forms; they do not have an **-s** form.) It is impossible to support the view of *could* as "the past tense" in any natural meaning of that phrase when we consider examples like:

I can't come today, but I could come tomorrow.

We have already seen in considering full verbs that "the past tense" can more usefully be seen as the remote form. We shall find this idea helpful in considering the individual modal auxiliaries in Chapter 14.

We have already noted that Palmer is of the opinion that a "basic meaning" for each individual modal cannot be determined. He does, however, believe that it is possible to search for a set of closely related meanings. There is, of course, no reason why a particular structural item should have a unique meaning. On the other hand, if there is an enormous range of alternative meanings it will be almost impossible for a listener to decode sufficiently rapidly to understand natural speech. Again, the best approach is to look for a single central meaning while at the same time accepting that this may involve recognising a number of marginal examples. It is, I think, impossible to find a single set of primary semantic characteristics for *should* (discussed on pages 123/5) which unites all of the following:

How should I know?
Who should come along but Bill!
Should anyone call, could you tell them I'll be back about four.
If one green bottle should accidently fall . . .
You should see a doctor!

This is, as Palmer has suggested, a messy area. The problem is not, however, anything like as difficult as certain grammar books make out. Thomson and Martinet (page 116) say:

> *May/might* can be used in conditional sentences
> instead of *will/would* to indicate a possible instead of a
> certain result:
> *If he sees you he will stop* (certain).
> *If he sees you he may stop* (possible).

This statement introduces a totally unnecessary complication. The difference between *will* and *may* in the examples given is exactly the same as the fundamental difference between those same two modal auxiliaries. Their occurrence "in conditional sentences" has nothing to do with the matter at all.

Similarly, Shepherd (*Ways to Grammar, Macmillan, 1984*) suggests unnecessary confusion in saying:

> Most modals have more than one meaning. For example, *may* is sometimes used to express *permission,* and sometimes to express *possibility.* Usually the meaning is clear from the situation or context.

Clearly, the communicative meaning will be different in different contexts. This does not, however, necessarily imply that *may* does not have a fundamental meaning. Communicative meaning is a combination of the primary semantic characteristics of a form and other factors.

Starting from the view that each modal has several meanings, it is exceptionally difficult to discern common ground. Starting with the assumption that each individual modal has a *single* meaning, though perhaps with an occasional eccentric or historical use, is much more fruitful. The meanings of the individual modal auxiliaries are discussed in detail in the next chapter. An example, however, clarifies certain points about the search for a single meaning:

I'm afraid I can't tell you.
Spaniards can't play football.
John can come.

All the examples contain certain ambiguities. The first suggests two para-phrases of quite different meaning: *I don't know* or *I have promised not to say anything.* The second example may be either the speaker expressing contempt for Spanish footballing skills or a newspaper headline announcing that the Spanish will be banned, or even that the game in which Spain is involved has been called off because the pitch is water-logged.

The ambiguities suggest that *can* has more than one meaning — ability, possibility, permission, etc. The ambiguities arise, however, from consider-ing the use of *can* in particular contexts. In fact, a constant underlying non-contextual meaning can be discerned.

Consider the example *John can come.* The underlying, general meaning of *can* is associated with possibility; ambiguity arises from different kinds of possibility; in this example the possibility of permission (the speaker allows John to come) or physical possibility (John's leg is better, he's able to walk again) or the possibility of non-restriction (John is free on the day in question). Usually the speaker's and listener's pre-knowledge and the context resolve the ambiguity. Essentially, however, unique non-contextual meanings can be identified for each individual modal auxiliary.

Another simple example with *can* illustrates this point further. If I say *You can't leave your car there* my contribution is to assert that it is not *poss-ible* to leave your car there; as listener, you may understand that it is not *physically* possible — the parking space is too small — but in other circumstances you will understand that I am telling you that we are in a no-parking area i.e. it is not *legally* possible. My (speaker's) reference is *always* to possibility; in different circumstances the listener interprets different kinds of possibility.

It is untrue to suggest that language, particularly in such a complex area, is totally regular. It is equally untrue, however, to suggest that it consists of an enormous number of random, unrelated items. Even in the complex area of the modal auxiliaries, there are powerful patterns which may be seen and understood, and which lead to a deeper understanding in individ-ual examples.

The 'must'/'have to' contrast

Sentences like:

I have to get the 8 o'clock train.
I must get the 8 o'clock train.

seem similar in meaning. While it is quite clear that

You don't have to get the 8 o'clock train.
You mustn't get the 8 o'clock train.

have quite different meanings.
It would be a very strange situation indeed if two sentences had identical meanings and when *not (n't)* was inserted into both, their meanings were quite different. The implication is clear — however similar the meaning of the first two sentences may appear, there must be a semantic difference. This is obvious in the second pair of examples, but exists equally in the first.

There is further evidence that *must* and *have to* are clearly distinct. It is, for example, possible to make the following transformation:

I have to catch the 8 o'clock train.
I had to catch the 8 o'clock train.

while a similar change is not possible with:
I must catch the 8 o'clock train.
unless the transformed sentence is also *I had to . . . .*

Finally, we note that the two can co-occur:

They must have had to catch a later train.
I think you must have to switch it on here first.

We have already dealt with the nature of the difficulty. *Must* is a basic modal auxiliary, but *(have) to* is not. The common characteristic of the modal auxiliaries is that they involve the speaker's *judgment*, or, perhaps better expressed in this context, the *speaker's* judgment.

In the case of *must* that judgment is about *necessity. (Have) to* is also about necessity. In this case, however, it is about some *objective* necessity. The necessity may be of different kinds, for example, logical or legal.

The difference between *must* and *(have) to* is thus clear — both are concerned with necessity; the former is subjective necessity, as perceived by the speaker, and the latter is *objective* necessity. This explanation immediately clarifies some difficulties; there is clearly little difference between:
I have to catch the 8.30 and *I must catch the 8.30.*
The first may be paraphrased *It is necessary for me to catch the 8.30,* while the second may be paraphrased *In the present circumstances I see it as necessary that I catch the 8.30.*
This closeness of meaning will always be the case in sentences with "I" as subject. With another subject the distinction is much clearer:

(1) *He has to have his hair cut.*
(2) *He must have his hair cut.*

can be paraphrased as:

1. *The rules say his hair must be cut/He has been told to have his hair cut.*
2. *I insist that he has his hair cut.*

If the necessity derives from some source external to the speaker *(have) to* is appropriate; if the source of the necessity is the speaker's own volition or perception, *must* is appropriate.
The co-occurence examples are now easy to explain. We may paraphrase *They must have had to get a later train* as:

Since they are not here yet, I assert that it is logically necessary that they took a later train; they would not do this unless it was necessary and I therefore conclude that it was necessary for them.

Mustn't and don't have to

Although:

You have to get the 8 o'clock train and *You must get the 8 o'clock train*

seem similar in meaning, the negatives are quite different:

You mustn't get the 8 o'clock train.   You don't have to get the 8 o'clock train.

We now see why this is.

You have to . . .   = *It is necessary for you to ...*
You don't have to . . .   = *It is not necessary for you to ...*

(Have) to is about objective necessity, the opposite of which is objective non-necessity. The negation belongs to the necessity.

With a modal auxiliary the situation is quite different.

You must get the 8.30	= *In the circumstances I believe it is necessary for you to (get the 8.30).*
You mustn't get the 8.30	= *In the circumstances I believe it is necessary for you to (not get the 8.30).*

The negation does not belong to the necessity, but to what follows. We may summarise:

Don't have to = it is not necessary that. . . You don't have to ask first.
Mustn't   = It is necessary not to . . . You mustn't forget to phone.

Interestingly, the distinction accounts for the existence of the form *had to*, and the fact that this appears to be the "past tense" equivalent of both *has/have to* and *must*. If the speaker looks back on a past event and refers to necessity, that necessity will be objective, not the subjective necessity "in the present circumstances", expressed by a modal auxiliary. Talking of tomorrow I may say *I must catch the 8.30* but referring factually to yesterday, when the necessity is objectified, *I had to catch the 8.30* will be obligatory.

Most *Must* is a modal auxiliary. Two of these cannot co-occur. All the sentences which contain another modal auxiliary in which the speaker expresses judgment about necessity contain *have to:*

You'll have to do something about that.
He must have had to stay late at the office.
Do you think they could have had to stay late?

Such examples clearly show the use of *have to;* the speaker judges the inevitability, desirability, possibility etc. of the (objective) necessity of the event. Such sentences provide further evidence for the fundamental distinction between *must* and *(have) to*.

Palmer discusses this distinction with reference to examples from the Survey of English Usage and asserts that:

> There are some contexts in which these verbs are interchangeable and seem not to differ at all in meaning. . . . One can, of course, insist that with *must* the speaker is in some way involved, even though his involvement may be minimal, but that can hardly be proved.

He goes on to suggest that rather than two kinds of necessity — subjective and objective, we really need three kinds — subjective, neutral and external and that we may say decisively that *have to* is never subjective, and *must* is never external (objective). By implication, he suggests some area of overlap in the area of "neutral necessity".

The two authentic examples from the Survey of English Usage which he quotes do not support this complicating idea. They are:

I must have an immigrant's visa. Otherwise they are likely to kick me out you see.
I've really got to know when completion is likely. Otherwise I might find myself on the street.

Clearly it is possible in the first example to say *I have to have an immigrant's visa* . . . . The difference of meaning is slight, but in this case (using *have to)* the speaker emphasises the necessity of the visa and the relationship between failure to follow the rules and the consequence (being thrown out). With the words the speaker actually used — *I must have* . . . the emphasis shifts from the abstract necessity of the visa, and the consequence, to the necessity *for the speaker* and the consequences *for the speaker.* The choice of *must* rather than *have to* in the first part of what the speaker says, has the effect of adding *to me* to the implied . . . *and I don't want that to happen.*

A similar analysis applies to the second example from the Survey. This time the speaker chooses *have to* to indicate he needs a completion date (for buying or selling a house) not simply so that he knows it, for himself, but because there is some external necessity to know — probably he has to tell somebody else otherwise they will take action and he "might find himself on the street".

With "I" as subject, in positive sentences, the difference will always be small. It would not be particularly surprising if some speakers had a strong personal preference for one rather than the other and if usage was not totally consistent in this area. Again, as so often in this book however, it is important to stress that the language is much more regular — indeed much simpler — than grammarians and teachers sometimes suggest.

The contrast with *'ll have to*

There is further evidence for contrast of meaning between *must* and *(have) to* if we consider:

You must wear a jacket.
You'll have to wear a jacket.
You have to wear a jacket.

It is easy to see that the first two are almost synonymous and that the second is closer than the third to the first. This is supported by analysis: *(have) to* is objective necessity; *'ll* is a modal auxiliary and therefore involves the speaker. If we add together the speaker's involvement, *('ll),* and the objective necessity of *(have) to,* we make a form close in meaning to *must* which expresses the speaker's view of necessity.

The explanations we have just considered throw light on the use of:

I'll have to be going (shortly/soon).
I (really) must go.

The first of these, used by a guest towards the end of a visit, is likely to prompt a remark from the host such as:

Oh, really. Would you like a cup of tea before you go?

It is extremely unlikely that the host will expect the guest to leave immediately. This is not surprising when we remember that the speaker has used a form *(be going)* which expresses the departure as an event extended in time, a process. The *'ll,* as discussed in the next chapter, expresses the immediacy of the process to the speaker.

The second example is much more likely to be taken as an indication of immediate departure and the difference becomes even clearer in an example such as:

A *Goodness, is that the time. I'm afraid I must go.*
B *Oh. would you like a cup of tea first?*
A *Thank you. I'm afraid I have to. The bus leaves in three minutes.*

Teachers frequently discuss the contrasts between *must* and *have to* and between *mustn't* and *don't have to*. Only rarely is attention drawn to *'ll have to*. This form is more frequent in everyday speech than either *must* or *have to*. Perhaps teachers need to give it more priority.

A classroom problem

Many students over-use *must* and avoid *have to* completely. This is partly because teachers frequently give examples beginning *I must* and, as we have seen there is little difference between the meaning of *I must* and *I have to*. Teachers can make the distinction clearer by presenting a wider range of examples — choosing some with an obvious outside agency, for example, traffic signs, and making sure they introduce examples with subjects other than "I".

Students are unlikely to be misunderstood if they confuse *must* and *have to* but they do need to know *(have) to* in order to make such sentences as *I had to wait 3 hours,* and the difference between *mustn't* and *don't have to* is essential. It is confusing to teach that the positive sentences are "almost the same" and the negatives "completely different". It is better to make the distinction clear from a relatively early stage in the teaching.

It is also essential to avoid statements about either of *must* and *have to* being "stronger" than the other. (I have seen the statement made both ways round in textbooks!). The "strength" of either form will depend upon its communicative meaning — this in turn depends on factors other than a simple choice of verb form. It is possible that "objective necessity" may be stronger if applied to "I" than any necessity I impose upon myself, using *must.* Equally, however, if *must* is given a heavy stress in speech, it is possible the necessity I impose upon myself appears stronger than any external necessity. The considerations are slightly different with second or third person subjects, but it still remains true that the communicative force ("strength") of the form is not constant.

What is constant, is that *must* is a modal auxiliary and is used, like the other modal auxiliaries, to express the speaker's perception at the moment of speaking.
(Have) to does not belong to the group of modal auxiliaries. It expresses not the speaker's (subjective) view of necessity, but objective necessity.

Must always carries an implication of the speaker's judgment; *(have) to* does not.

Summary

The basic group of modal auxiliaries is:

can, could, may, might, shall, should, will, would, must.

It is particularly important to note *will* and *shall* are included in this list, while forms with *(have) to* and *ought to* are not.

These modal auxiliaries:

a. Form a closed group of words sharing structural and semantic properties. It is not helpful to see them as "defective verbs".

b. They are essentially grounded in the moment of speaking — based on an assessment "in the present circumstances".

c. They express the speaker's (or, in questions, listener's) judgment about the non-factual, non-temporal elements in an action.

It is clear that these theoretical insights have little immediate relevance to the language teaching classroom. We shall, however, see in the next chapter where the primary semantic characteristics of the individual modal auxiliaries are considered, that the insights do have important practical applications.

14. The Individual Modal Auxiliaries

In the previous chapter we saw that the modal auxiliaries have in common that each involves the speaker's or listener's judgment. Each one may be paraphrased as "In the present circumstances, it seems to me XXX that . . ." The XXX will be different for each individual modal auxiliary and, as we have already seen, will involve such ideas as possibility and necessity. In each case the speaker refers to a non-factual state as possible, necessary etc. The speaker's judgment is exercised precisely at the moment of speaking — the modal auxiliaries are intrinsically grounded in the present moment.

This contrasts with the traditional view that certain modal auxiliaries were "the past tense" of others (*can/could, will/would, shall/should, may/ might*). With full verbs we have found it is necessary to generalise the concept of "the past tense", recognising remote forms. It is natural to ask whether the approach will work for those modal auxiliaries traditionally thought of as "the past tense". The answer is *Yes*, and two ideas we have met already support this.

It is clear that *could* has no past time reference in *I can't come today but I could come tomorrow.* It is also scarcely surprising that students who have been taught that *could* is "the past" find such sentences confusing. Equally, it is easy to see that *I could come* is more remote than *I can come.* Similar considerations apply to *He may/might be there.* One or two examples of this kind certainly do not prove that the concept of remoteness is a useful one, but they at least suggest it may be worth further exploration.

In the last chapter we noted the apparent anomaly that *must* did not possess a "past tense" equivalent. As soon as we note that this is not "a past tense", but the more general remote form it is easy to see why this is so. *Must* refers to the speaker's perception of necessity, and as soon as the speaker recalls an event in Past Time where something was necessary, that necessity becomes objective. For this reason *had to* describes all necessity in Past Time. The intrinsic meaning of *must* does not admit the concept of remoteness. This being so, no form exists to express that concept in English.

We turn now to the search for the meaning of the individual modal auxiliaries. The treatment is necessarily brief, and tries only to identify the primary semantic charcteristic of each. It must be emphasised that the discussion here is intended to deepen the reader's understanding, and is not intended initially to have anything to do with language teaching. The question of how these forms are best presented in the classroom is referred to later (see page 126).

Can/could

These are best dealt with as a pair, and we may state simple paraphrases as follows:

Can = I assert that it is possible that . . .
Could = I assert that it is "remotely" possible that. . .

These are the general, underlying meanings of *can* and *could*. Different kinds of "possibility" exist, and will be interpreted in different contexts. Before a recent world athletic championships a newspaper headline read:

OVETT CANNOT
REPLACE COE

Several interpretations are possible:

(1) The writer does not think Ovett is good enough to replace Coe.

(2) Something, perhaps injury, prevents Ovett replacing Coe.

(3) Ovett is prevented by somebody — perhaps the Official Games Committee — from replacing Coe.

(4) Coe will not allow Ovett to replace him.

Only an understanding of who Coe and Ovett are, the situation prevailing at the time, the rules of international athletics, etc. permit the headline to be interpreted unambiguously. It is, nonetheless, apparent that each interpretation depends upon a different "possibility".

Uses of *could* are invariably possibilities of a more remote kind than uses of *can*. The "remoteness" may be remoteness in time, social relationship, or likelihood:

I could ride a bike when I was a kid but I haven't done it for years. (Time)
Could you pass the salt please? (Relationship)
He could be a foreigner, but I don't think so. (Likelihood)

Can always refers to different kinds of possibility. *Could* is also about possibility, but is more remote than can. The possibility may be of different kinds:

Can you swim?	Ability.
I can't lift this.	Objective impossibility.
You can't smoke in here.	Possibility decided by rules.
Can you remind me tomorrow please.	Requests *(Is it possible for you to . . .?)*
Can I give you a lift?	Offers *(Is it possible for me to . . . for you).*
He can't be French.	Deduction — logical possibility. (always with *can't*).
I'm afraid I couldn't get tickets.	Impossibility in the past — remote in time.
Could you pass the salad please.	Polite request — remote relationship.
You could have left it at home.	Remote, logical possibility.

Functionally, the contextual meaning of individual examples may differ greatly. At the same time, the primary semantic characteristics of the forms remain constant.

May/might

In general *may* is a relatively rare word in contemporary English. It remains common in *May I have another?* but rarer in *You may have one if you like.* It is still relatively common in examples like:

He may be French.
They may have lost their way.
She may come.

In the case of the last group of examples, if *may* is replaced by *might,* the contrast resembles that between *could* and *can;* the examples with *might* are in some sense more remote. The idea that *might* is the remote form of *may* is supported by the naturalness of both of:

May I suggest the veal?   *Might I suggest the veal?*

coupled with the implication that the latter will sound more natural if *Sir/ Madam* is added; there is a distinct feeling that this use is appropriate in situations of remote relationship, resembling uses of *could* such as *Could I suggest Thursday, the 14th.*
    This view of the *may/might* contrast is supported by the naturalness of *May I have one?* and the fact that *Might I have one?* although not impossible, appears strange. The form is clearly requesting direct, immediate permission so that an immediate, rather than remote, form is more likely.
    It is clear that in many situations there is a close similarity of meaning between all of *can, could, may, might:*

He can be French.   *Can I smoke?*
He could be French.   *Could I smoke?*
He may be French.   *May I smoke?*
He might be French.   *Might I smoke?*

It is immediately apparent that in each example *possibility* is implied. At the same time the examples are by no means interchangeable. Many British children will recall asking parents *Can I . . .?* only to be told *You can, but you may not.*

The *can/may* contrast is readily apparent in the pair:

Can I smoke here?   *May I smoke here?*

The first suggests *Is it allowed?* the second suggests *Do you permit me?*
The difference is that with *can/could* the speaker perceives the existence of a possibility; with *may/might* the speaker is volitionally involved in the creation of a possibility.
This explains the contrast and such (relatively rare) contemporary uses as *You may go now,* and *He may come* (in the meaning *I will allow him to*).
A source of some confusion is that different kinds of possibility may be associated with *can* and *may* in contrastive examples:

It $\begin{vmatrix} \text{does} \\ \text{can} \\ \text{may} \end{vmatrix}$ not mean that. . .

It does not . . . is a statement of pure fact. With *It cannot . . .,* the speaker is involved in a judgment about the possibility, but not in the creation of the possibility. With *It may not . . .* the temptation is to say that this is "not as strong as *cannot*". Contextually this is true — but why? The point is that *may* involves the speaker personally in the creation of the possibility. In this particular context this can only mean that it is the speaker's assessment of possibility and, therefore, that that assessment may be at fault and, therefore, it is less decisive than *cannot*.

Nobody would suggest that this kind of conscious perception, the selection of particular primary semantic characteristics, is involved. Nor would it be sensible to introduce such considerations into the average language teaching situation. It is, however, reassuring to find that the language behaves much more consistently than is often believed.

Having looked at the examples above, the reader should have no difficulty in seeing that two different kinds of possibility are involved in *Stephen can give you a lift*, and *Stephen may give you a lift*. Contextually, the first would be seen as an offer. Since the speaker announces the existence of the possibility, it would only be natural to do so if it was of interest to the listener and that will only be true if the sentence is functionally an offer. The second sentence, in contrast, suggests a meaning something like "It is logically possible for Stephen . . .". It is only discussing logical possibilities, not stating the existence of a definite possibility. It will be seen as a speculation, not an offer.

He may come may imply the granting of permission, or a prediction. In contemporary English it is much more likely to be the latter. Nonetheless, if we contrast *He can come* and *He may come* it becomes clear that the meanings may be paraphrased *It is possible for him to come* and *I suppose it is possible that he will come*. The difference is apparent; the *may* example involves the speaker explicitly in the possibility. It is this which is the defining contrast between *may* and *can* — the fact that the speaker is explicitly involved in the "creation" of the possibility. We may paraphrase *may* as:

May = If I have anything to do with it, it is possible that. . .

This paraphrase is cumbersome, but does, as we shall see, reflect an important distinction common to several definitions within the group of modal auxiliaries. The definition of *might* is similar, with the additional idea of remoteness.

Must

As we saw in the previous chapter, this may be paraphrased:

Must = I assert that it is necessary that . . .

The necessity may be of different kinds, for example, legal, moral, practical or logical:

You mustn't leave the car there after six.
You mustn't say things like that to Mrs. Wilson.
You must be careful with your money there.
They must have got the letter by now.

Will, Would, Shall, Should

We turn now to the area of greatest potential confusion. We have already seen that the *will/shall* distinction has been confused by misguided teaching and that the whole problem of *will/shall* as "the future" has been misrepresented.

With all of these modal auxiliaries a further problem arises; there is a contrast between the reduced and non-reduced form in statements:

I'll be going.	*I'd be surprised.*
I will be going.	*I would be surprised.*
I shall be going.	*I should be surprised.*

The question forms with the reduced form are not, however, possible.

There are occasions when we cannot be sure if a reduced form *('ll* or *'d)* represents *shall/will* or *should/would,* or even whether it may be an independent form.

In language teaching, contrasts such as *should/would* have frequently been taught. This has often created further confusion.

Perhaps surprisingly in these circumstances of apparent general confusion, providing we bear in mind the Principle of General Use, we shall find that primary semantic characteristics may be identified for each of these auxiliaries and that consistent patterns may be discerned. The principal difficulty arises in identifying the characteristics for one; that done, the relationships between them are relatively straightforward.

Will

Will is not uniquely associated with Future Time, although most uses do refer to Future Time. Here are some examples:

(1) *I'll see him on Sunday.*
(2) *It's warm in here, I think I'll open the window.*
(3) *We'll have to do something about it.*
(4) *I'm sure they'll be home by now.*
(5) *What will you do if that doesn't work.*
(6) *It'll soon be 7 o'clock.*
(7) *He will keep ringing me early in the morning.*
(8) *Medicine will have taken great strides before the end of the century.*

We know that one common characteristic of the modals is shared by *will;* it relates to a state which is not factual for the speaker at the moment of speaking. It is, however, *psychologically immediate* for the speaker at the moment of speaking. The meaning may be loosely expressed as "given the present situation, and my perception of it, the situation to which I am referring must inevitably also be true". Two states are relevant — that pertaining at the moment of speaking, and a second one to which the speaker is referring; the two are, as the speaker sees them, inevitably linked.

We see immediately why *will* is strongly associated with reference to Future Time; the speaker refers to *two* states — that pertaining at the moment of speaking, and a second *which is seen as non-factual.* If two states are involved, there is a difference between them. The most common reason for that difference will be difference in time. If the state referred to is not seen by the speaker as factual, it is unlikely (though not impossible) for it to be in Past Time or Present Time; almost always it will be in Future Time. If it is *not* in Future Time the second state must be something of which the speaker does not have direct factual knowledge. Verb phrases of this kind containing *will* refer to logical inevitability, as in examples like *They will be there by now* (given the present time, the time they left, and my knowledge of the journey, the statement *They are there* must, inevitably, be true).

It is important to remember that the speaker may be mistaken, or expressing a personal view with which the hearer disagrees — it is not that the condition referred to *is* necessarily true, but that the speaker asserts that, given *his* perception of the situation, the situation must inevitably *arise* or *be true*. The *or* here is significant; the implication of the word *arise* is that the second state will be true at a later point in time — *arise* refers to *will* used with Future Time reference; *be true* refers to uses of *will* where the connection between the two states is logical, rather than temporal.

We have now reached a definition of *will;* given my, the speaker's, perception of a state or set of circumstances, which is psychologically immediate for me at the moment of speaking, I conclude that a second state is, or will be, necessarily also true.

If we wish to state this in the form suggested for the other modal auxiliaries it would be:

will = Given my perception of the immediate situation, it is inevitably true that...

These (alternative) definitions solve a number of problems which produce so-called exceptions in the traditional approach.

It is clear that questions with *Will I . . .?* will be unusual; their meaning would be *Do you assert, given the present circumstances, that it is inevitable that I . . . ?* In general the person addressed is unlikely to see the speaker's actions as inevitable. Interestingly, however, such examples are possible — perhaps as a commentary supplied by a stage performer such as a magician to accompany his routine: *Will I find it under this cup . . . ?*

It is easy to see why this example — superficially "an exception" — is possible. If the magician is involved in a *routine,* then it follows an inevitable path and the observers, aware of this, may perceive "inevitability". Questions such as:

Will I annoy you if I put the TV on?
Will I ever finish?

are also possible, though unusual. It is clear why — the first discusses an inevitable consequence of putting the TV on, the second is a rhetorical remark, suggesting that the speaker is unsure that the inevitable will occur — hence the connotational force of *Will I ever . . . ?*

Examples such as *Will I get one for you?* which are not associated with inevitability, however, seem unnatural. Usage in this area is not standard throughout Britain. Many Scottish and Irish speakers of English naturally prefer *Will I open the window?* to the corresponding question with *Shall.* Such regional variations do occur, but do not invalidate the general and widely applicable descriptions discussed in this book.

Will will be common in statements about the speaker, or about objective fact, but relatively rare in the construction *You will . . .* This usage does, however, exist:

(1) *You will be met at the airport and taken direct to our office.*
(2) *You will be there by 7 o'clock.*

(1) suggests "Don't worry, arrangements have been made, you can rely on them". The person is reassured of the inevitability, and therefore reliability, of the arrangement.

(2) is ambiguous and has the following interpretations:
i. The train gets there in plenty of time — don't worry, there's no way you're going to be late.
ii. I insist that you are there by 7 o'clock whether you like it or not.

but both interpretations carry connotations of "inevitability", though for different reasons. The context will resolve the ambiguity. The use of *will* is consistent.

It is easy to see why *will* has come to be thought of as "the future". The "inevitability" of the situation may be temporal or logical. The former is much the more frequent. For this reason the majority of sentences containing *will* relate to Future Time. The fact that a usage is highly frequent does not, however, justify us in *identifying* it with the form.

The unstressed *'ll* may be associated with "weak inevitability", which in turn, with Future Time reference, closely suggests an approximation to "the future as fact". It is clear that *They'll be pleased* may be contrasted with *I'm sure they'll be pleased* or *They **will** be pleased*. Each of the alternatives strengthens the initial utterance. The addition of *I'm sure* is similar in connotation to the extra stress on *will*. This does little more than make explicit the degree of inevitability associated with both the weak form, *'ll* and *will*.

Will with Future Time reference

We have already met three verb forms which may refer to Future Time:

(1) I think it's going to rain.
(2) I'm playing tennis on Saturday.
(3) We leave from Paddington.

Each of these forms is non-modal; the speaker expresses a view of the future event as *fact*. In (3) it is "pure fact", associated with those things entirely outside the speaker's control. In (1) and (2), which are aspectual forms, the speaker provides an interpretation of the temporal elements. In the case of (2) some action pre-dates Now which the speaker sees as linked to the future event; in (1) the speaker looks forward on the basis of evidence available at the moment of speaking.

Forms containing *will* or *'ll* are modal; they involve the speaker's *judgment* of the non-factual elements of a situation. Forms which relate to Future Time involve the speaker judging the situation which prevails at the moment of speaking and making a prediction on the basis of an immediate, instantaneous, perception of the situation at the moment of speaking.

This is remarkably similar in many cases to the *(be) going to* future. The distinction, though slight, is that the evidence associated with *(be) going to* futures tends to be cumulative — it has been available for some time. *Will* is more associated with the speaker's *instantaneous* perception at the moment of speaking. This becomes clear if we contrast the pair:

What are you going to do when you leave school?
What will you do when you leave school?

The first suggests that the person addressed will have thought about it earlier, and is now being asked to describe earlier plans; the second suggests that the speaker (questioner) believes the listener has not considered it before and is now being asked to give an instantaneous reaction to the question.

Will may be seen in two ways:

(i) A non-factual state seen by the speaker as "inevitable" given the state prevailing at the moment of speaking.
(ii) A state which is pyschologically immediate for the speaker although not known factually.

On different occasions one or other of these alternative descriptions of *will* is slightly more convenient. Both involve the speaker's immediate perception of the situation at the point Now.

The full (stressed) form *will* with Future Time reference suggests "this event is inevitable if the world continues on its present course". The weak form *'ll* may be taken to mean this event is "weakly inevitable". It is clear that the concept of "weak inevitability" begins to approximate to the concept of "the future as fact".

Two common uses of *will/'ll* illustrate this point. The form is common in speech for casual observations by the speaker about himself or herself:

Gosh it's warm in here, I think I'll open the window.
I'll just ring Jack before we go out.

These examples do not suggest previous planning, a previous arrangement, previous evidence, or any of the features associated with the other form. They do, on the other hand, suggest something over which the speaker has control and which involve a personal decision.

The *'ll* form is particularly common in conditional sentences:

I'll ask him if I see him.
You'll get wet unless you wait a few moments/if you go out now.

The speaker can never be quite sure that the event (s)he is describing is inevitable — nothing about the future is totally certain. This is reflected in the fact that many statements containing *'ll* are qualified by a condition, or words such as *probably, maybe, I think,* or said in contexts which supply "situational conditions": *I'll go if you will. Don't do that — you'll break it!* Sometimes the speaker "weakens" the statement in advance: *If I'm not mistaken, there'll be trouble about this!*

"The Future Continuous"

It remains to consider examples such as:

I'll be leaving tomorrow.

We have noted that the primary semantic characteristics *always* contribute in the same way to the total meaning of a complex verb phrase. This form contains *'ll* and a *(be)* + . . .*ing* form. Its meaning, therefore, arises from the combination of the meanings of these two factors. It is helpful to contrast:

I'll write to her tomorrow.
I'll be writing to her tomorrow.

The first suggests an instantaneous decision to write while the second suggests that although it has just become relevant to mention the fact, something pre-dates Now which allows me to say that the writing is inevitable. The second example is used typically if I write regularly so that I would write even if the present discussion were not taking place. The two elements of the explanation are present — the speaker sees an event which pre-dates the moment of speaking (the regularity of writing) which requires the *(be)* + . . .*ing* form; at the moment of speaking the event, although not factual, becomes psychologically immediate for the speaker — hence an *'ll* form.

There is a clear difference of connotational meaning between *Will you go?* and *Will you be going?* This is apparent if we analyse each according to component factors.

The second contains both *will* and *(be)* + . . .*ing*. It should, therefore, have connotations both of the listener's immediate perception *and* an event preceding Now. It is easy to see that with *both* of these elements the implication will be very strongly one of "the future as a matter of course" which is the name often given in traditional textbooks to forms of this kind.

In context, forms which contain both *(be)* + . . .*ing* and *will/'ll*, because of the implication of the event pre-dating the moment of speaking, tend to suggest greater certainty.

The Future in the Future

In theory *will* and *(be) going to* may combine to form examples such as:

I'll be going to see him as soon as he comes out of hospital.

Consideration of the circumstances in which this would be appropriate show how the elements of meaning contributed by the factors fit together. The *'ll* expresses the psychological immediacy for the speaker, while the looking forward is expressed by the *(be) going to* form. In fact, Palmer observes that although such forms may in theory exist, he noted no example in the Survey of English Usage.

Will — A Summary

Will does not refer to an event seen by the speaker as a matter of fact. Being a modal auxiliary, *will* necessarily expresses a relationship between *two* states, that prevailing at the time of speaking, and a second state. In the case of *will* this second state is:

1. *psychologically immediate* for the speaker and

2. seen as *inevitably linked* to the state prevailing at the moment of speaking.

Usually, the "inevitable linking" is in time, in which case *will* refers to events in Future Time. Occasionally, the inevitable linking is logical, in which case *will* may refer to events not in Future Time.

Shall

Many native speakers will recall being taught:

"*Shall* in the first person
Will in the second and third persons
The other way round if strong emphasis is needed."

This rule is nonsense. It is true that certain collocations are more frequent than others. This is explained, however, by the intrinsic difference in meaning between *shall* and *will*.

It is clear that *will* and *shall* are similar in meaning. They are not, however, identical. The contrast is similar to the one we have already met with *can/may*. *Shall* has the meaning of *will* and the additional meaning "if it's anything to do with me (the speaker)". In questions, of course, the implication becomes "if it's anything to do with you (the listener)".

It is immediately apparent that the construction *Shall you . . .* will very rarely be appropriate — the listener is involved through the *you.*

Shall is a relatively uncommon word in modern spoken English, although common in the constructions:

Shall I get one for you?
Shall we go tomorrow evening?

It is rare in all spoken statements but remains an important part of written legal English: *The initial capital of the Partnership shall belong to the Parties in equal shares and the profits and losses of the Partnership shall be borne by the Parties in equal shares.*

It is also common (usually in its archaic form) in the Ten Commandments: *Thou shalt not kill.*

There is a temptation to think that such legal and religious uses may be examples of linguistic fossils. Examination shows, however, that these uses of *shall* share a common meaning with more common examples from the spoken language — namely, the explicit involvement of the speaker in the creation of the "inevitability". This is self-evidently the case in legal usage in a contract where the situation described will arise because the signatories to the contract have chosen to create that situation. In the case of the Ten Commandments the involvement of the "speaker" becomes overt in a usage such as *Thou shalt not kill, says the Lord.*

The pattern is clear — *shall* is appropriate (for those British native speakers of English who use both *shall* and *will)* when the speaker's direct involvement in the creation of the inevitability is involved.

The *shall/will* contrast is clearly shown by the pair:

What time will we arrive?   What time shall we arrive?

The first invites the listener's opinion of what, given the present circumstances, is inevitable. The question would be appropriate during a journey from a passenger to the driver — *You know the situation, please give me the information.* With *shall,* the listener is involved in the creation of the inevitability. The question suggests *What time do you think it is appropriate for us to arrive?* Two people are discussing arrangements for a future event. It is a precisely the "if it's anything to do with you" element of the meaning of *shall* which is the source of these two very different interpretations.

Shall = According to my perception of the present situation, it is, if it's anything to do with me, inevitable that. . .

On one occasion Margaret Thatcher, then British Prime Minister, said under political pressure concerning the deployment of nuclear missiles in Britain *We shall deploy on time, unless the Russians. . .*

The implication is clear — it is the Prime Minister speaking, who perceives it as within her individual power to effect the deployment of the missiles. The use of *shall* rather than *will,* expresses her personal commitment to the action.

There is a popular protest song to which the old fashioned rule most certainly does not apply (*will* in the first person if special emphasis is needed) but which is covered by the description above — *We Shall Overcome.*

If we take the meaning of *shall* to involve the speaker in the creation of the inevitability, it is easy to see that this song expresses the personal commitment of each individual singer to the objectives of the group. The meaning conveys precisely the difference between *shall* and *will*.

The unstressed form

Sometimes teachers and students wonder whether *'ll* is "short for *shall* or *will*". The confusion of spoken/written and stressed/unstressed forms has already been discussed. It is by no means obvious that *'ll* is short for either *shall* or *will*. It is possible that *'ll* is an independent form and is beginning to assume the role of "the pure future" in English.

The reader may have noted, however, that in the discussion above it has been assumed that *'ll*, if it is short for anything, is short for *will*. There is a reason for this. Although rare, the full stressed form *shall* does occur in positive sentences. It also has a weak form, (ʃəl). There seems no reason to assume that it has a second weak (or weaker!) form *'ll*. For this reason, *'ll* is treated as a weak form of *will*. It is also clear that if *'ll* expresses what is seen by the speaker as "weakly inevitable", the difference between involvement and non-involvement will also be considerably weakened. In short, the question of whether *'ll* is an unstressed form of *shall* or *will* becomes meaningless.

Shall in the classroom

As we noted *shall* is rare in modern spoken English. For most school students it will be sufficient for them to know the *shall* in first person questions and perhaps in the fixed phrase *Let's . . . , shall we*. In all other cases they can, almost without risk, use *will*. The *shall/will* distinction is certainly not a matter which deserves more than a few moments of classroom time during a student's whole school career.

Would

At first sight there is little to link usages such as:

I wouldn't think so.
I would if I could.
We would always go there picnicking, when I was a child.

Would is clearly related to *will* and the relationship is by now a familiar one — *would* is "a remote form" of *will*. This is clearly the case with examples such as:

Would you open the window please? (remoteness of relationship)

I will if I can.
I would if I could.   (remoteness of likelihood/possibility).

Like the other modal auxiliaries, *would* involves a non-factual interpretation of the situation. As we have seen, *will* expresses a state which is psychologically immediate for the speaker, and arises out of a perception of the present circumstances. We might then expect *would* to express an event which is *psychologically remote* for the speaker. This is exactly the use of *would*. This emerges clearly in examples such as *I would be surprised*, or *I would never have expected that to happen.*

The distinction is more difficult to see, but more revealing, in the contrast between:

We went there a lot when I was a child.
We would go there a lot when I was a child.

The first is a statement of fact. In context, the second carries an implication of nostalgia. This arises from the primary semantic characteristics of *would* which expresses the speaker's personal, *psychological* rather than factual, remoteness from the event at the moment of speaking.

The distinction between the factual quality of the remote form, and the non-factuality of *would* is further demonstrated by contrasts such as:

I didn't realise he was here.
I didn't realise he would be here.

Was suggests my *knowledge* was wrong, whereas *would be* suggests my imagination or judgment of the situation was inaccurate. It is the psychological element in the semantic charateristics of *would* which is the source of this distinction.

The meaning of *would* is clear; it has the association of "inevitability" which we saw with *will* but with an important difference; *will* is based on *two* situations — one which is psychologically immediate for the speaker at the moment of speaking, and the second, the event or state which is seen as "inevitably" linked. In the case of *would,* the first perceived state is, at the moment of speaking, remote from the speaker, in a non-factual way. This cumbersome expression is seen to be equivalent to the fact that the speaker, at the moment of speaking, conceptualises the action as *hypothetical,* i.e. non-factually remote.

Would = Given the (hypothetical) situation which I perceive at the moment of speaking, the action described is also inevitably true.

English does not possess a "conditional tense". It is, however, common for *would* to occur in sentences containing conditionals and not unusual for it to be presented in textbooks under headings such as "the conditional". Once more it is necessary to remind ourselves of the Principle of General Use. *Would* is not "the conditional". It does, however, frequently co-occur with conditions. It is easy to see why this is so. *Would* is associated with events which are "hypothetical" for the speaker; in this context "hypothetical" means "true in certain circumstances, not those currently prevailing". This immediately suggests the question *In what circumstances?* The speaker, anticipating this implied question, frequently makes those circumstances explicit in the form of a clause beginning with such words as *when, if,* or *unless.*The fundamental meaning of *would* is such that it naturally occurs in sentences containing explicit conditions.
Examples such as:

I would expect him to be very pleased to see you.
I would expect so.

are perhaps the clearest examples of the general use of *would.* The speaker *creates* a hypothetical quality to the situation and, in doing so, automatically distances himself from the factual quality of the statement. I recently came across a particularly noteworthy example. The then British Foreign Secretary interviewed on television was asked:

Interviewer *Is Britain supplying arms to the Afghan rebels?*
F. Secretary *I have no knowledge of that.*
Interviewer *Do you believe they have sufficient arms?*
F. Secretary *I would imagine that they would need more.*

This is not "a conditional"; it is, however, immediately apparent that the speaker is deliberately making clear that his remark is *not* a statement of fact. *Would* emphasises the non-factual nature of the remark.

Questions beginning *Would you . . .?* are common, and frequently presented in classroom teaching as "polite forms". Such contextual explanations do not define the forms. In fact, *Would you . . .?* questions contrast with the more direct *Do you . . .?* They:

(i) are distanced "from the speaker".
(ii) refer to the perception of the listener at the moment of speaking.

These two defining qualities make clear the differences in contrasts like:

Do you like tea?   *Are you interested in a ticket?*
Would you like a cup of tea?   *Would you be interested in a ticket?*

In general we see that *would* expresses a situation which, at the moment of speaking, is psychologically remote from the speaker (hypothetical) but has the suggestion of inevitability associated with *will*.

Should

We come now to a much less tidy modal auxiliary. Palmer said that the area is messy, and that any attempt to argue for a single central meaning is doomed to failure. Swan has remarked that any attempt to find a single meaning results in cases of special pleading. With *should,* this is definitely so.
There is no doubt that *should* has more than one use:

(1) Should it rain, the game will be postponed until Saturday.
(2) It doesn't seem fair that he should get away without paying.
    It's funny you should say that.
(3) How should I know!
(4) It's about 5 miles, I should think.
    It must be about quarter past four, I should say.
(5) If you should bump into him, please tell him I'm looking for him.
    If one green bottle should accidently fall . . . . (a popular song).
(6) We were just talking about it when who should come along but Sandra.
(7) You should have taken your coat.
    I don't think he should have done that.

It is immediately clear than any attempt to identify the primary semantic characteristics of *all* uses of *should* is doomed to failure. Some of these examples at least must be "a different *should*". This should not surprise us. Such closed-class grammatical items as *there* and *one* evidently have more than one use. *(There* is both an adverb of place, and, quite distinctly, a pronoun). The contention of this book is not that the language is *totally* regular, but that within the verb the majority of forms are part of a basic and completely regular structure.

Returning to *should,* we expect it to form some kind of relationship with *would* and *will/shall.* We might expect *should*:

(i) To express a non-factual state, psychologically remote or distant from the speaker at the moment of speaking.

(ii) To include the hypothetical idea associated with *would*.

(iii) Like *shall*, to include the idea "if it's anything to do with me".

(iv) To express *two* states in contrast with each other — that pertaining at the moment of speaking, in contrast to a second state which has the characteristics (i) to (iii).

Shall, as we have seen, may be expressed informally as "this will happen if it's anything to do with me". We then expect *should* to mean "this would happen if it was anything to do with me". This, in turn, may be paraphrased more simply as *I think it is desirable that. . . .* Clearly, this is exactly the underlying meaning of *should* in examples like:

You should have brought your swimming things.
We really should tell your father.
Should we try and catch the early train?

In examples such as *He should be there by now,* the choice of *should* suggests the speaker's direct involvement, and therefore "as far as I can see, it is reasonable to assume. . .". This use parallels other uses within the modal auxiliary group such as the speaker's involvement in the creation of possibility with the use of *may*.

The semantics of *would*, and the *should/would* distinction are exemplified by the examples:

I think so.   *I would think so.*   *I should think so!*

Other uses of 'should'

It is not possible to identify a single use of *should*. Apart from its full modal auxiliary use, in which its meaning relates closely to those of *would* and *will/shall*, the following distinct uses may be identified:

a. To express weak probability

If you should see her, could you tell her I'm looking for her please.
If he should arrive while I'm out, will you ask him to wait a moment please.
Should it rain, the game will be postponed until tomorrow.

b. In 'that' clauses

There are a number of constructions, all beginning with *that* which contain a distinct use of *should*.

I was delighted that he should recognise me after so long.
I am amazed (that) anyone should think like that.
The lawyers recommended that we should take no further action.

This use of *should* never occurs in a main clause, always in a subordinate clause introduced by *that*.

c. I should say/think/imagine

This item is non-generative — it would be impossible, for example, to make **She should say*. These items are now fixed phrases in the language, lexical items, meaning "to the best of my knowledge, as far as I know".

d. With 'How' and 'Why'

The two expressions:
How should I know!
Why should I (tell you)!
are fairly frequent in the spoken language. Frequently they express the speaker's irritation.

It may be noted that there is an underlying similarity of meaning of the *shoulds* referred to in **a, b, c,** In each case there is reference to "in circumstances other than those prevailing at the moment". In other words, these uses of *should* all express hypothetical situations.

Unfortunately, even this restricted area of common ground does not apply to examples such as:

Then, guess what — who should come along but John himself.
I didn't know at the time that I should see him again.

The last example is certainly now old-fashioned, and in contemporary English *was going to* would almost certainly be preferred. Even so, it is clear that *should* is a complex, and indeed "messy" area.

There is even further confusion waiting. Some native speakers were taught in school the curious *shall/will* rule referred to earlier. In a similar way the teaching of a very doubtful "rule" has caused further confusion with *should* and *would*. Both words are common in relatively formal written English, and in particular, in business correspondence. Many secretarial courses teach students that it is "bad style" to repeat the same word in the same or consecutive sentences.

The result is that a sentence such as *I would be grateful if you would . . .,* will frequently be "improved", to *I should be grateful if you would. . . .*
The reader is reminded of the experiment referred to on page 43. In no single case was there complete agreement about the possibilities. Even if we "explain away" one or two of the people as making strange choices, it is clear that there was no general agreement upon a basic pattern.

Should — A Summary

Each of the modal auxiliaries we have met so far has had a set of primary semantic characteristics which can be identified and which apply to all uses of that auxiliary. This is not possible with *should*. *Should* does have a modal auxiliary use which parallels the other modal auxiliaries discussed in this chapter. In addition, a number of other uses may be identified. It is necessary to treat these separately. These separate uses include:

a. The conditional use, *If he should come. . .* or *Should he come. . .*

b. The use in subordinate clauses preceded by *that.*

c. *How/why should . . . .*

d. Comments, *I should think/say.*

e. The old-fashioned use now usually replaced by *was going to.*

f. *Who should walk in . . . .*

It is immediately clear that this area is a minefield for language teachers and students but careful thought shows the problem is not as difficult as it at first appears.

The modal auxiliaries do form a group. They are used consistently. This applies to *should* as to all others. In addition, *should* has a number of additional uses, which need to be studied separately. Few students are confused by the fact that *there* or *one* have more than one use; there is no reason why *should* should be a source of confusion if its various uses are separated and identified.

Teaching the modal auxiliaries

Certain of the modal auxiliaries are notorious areas of difficulty in teaching and learning English. Many of these difficulties are generated by teachers bringing together unsuitable areas, thereby creating confusion. The most important point for teachers is, therefore, to try to avoid this.

Recently, language teaching has been strongly influenced by the Communicative Approach. This approach can, sensibly applied, help to simplify the presentation and study of the modal auxiliaries. A functional presentation which highlights the contextual uses of individual modals will, for a majority of school students, avoid areas of difficulty.

Can/could

There is little difficulty in presenting *can/could*, providing the general concept of remote forms has been introduced.

The idea of *could* as "a polite form" can cause confusion without the framework provided by the concept of 'remote relationship'.

May/might

May is relatively rare. It is probably best taught in two *separate* stages:
(i) In the request form *May I . . . ?* where it is contrasted with *Can I . . . ?* making the distinction that the former question involves the personal decision of the listener.
(ii) In statements, with the meaning "as far as I am concerned it is possible that". This differs from *can* because of the "as far as I am concerned".

Most students will need only one use of *might* — "it is quite likely that". A few students may find useful the lexical item *Might I suggest . . . .*

Shall/will

For the vast majority of school students the information they need about *shall/will* and *'ll* is very limited. From the classroom point of view it is probably sufficient to tell them:

Use *shall* in first person questions.
Use *'ll* in all neutral statements.
Use *will* on all occasions when the full form is necessary, (questions, tags, etc.) except first person questions.

The main discussion must be of *will* (and *'ll*) in contrast to other ways of talking about Future Time.

Should/would

The main area of confusion is very often the *should/would* contrast. It is, unfortunately, common for teachers to raise the question *What is the difference between 'should' and 'would'?* This is most unhelpful. I can think of no circumstances in which it is helpful to contrast the pair *should/would* (and that pair alone) for students. It is more probably true to say that there is no single area of English which is more likely to cause unnecessary confusion for students.

For school students it seems best to present *particular* uses of one *or* the other in any one lesson. For those at the upper end of the school English course or in higher education it may be helpful to gather *all* uses of one *or* the other together to search for the underlying similarity of meaning in uses of either *should* or *would.*

For advanced students it may be helpful to look at sorting and describing practices which will contrast various modal auxiliaries with each other. Such practices will concern themselves not only with the *should/would* contrast, but with the much more general problem of the boundaries of meaning between various pairs of modal auxiliaries. The practice of contrasting the single pair *should/would* is, however, particularly unhelpful.

Teachers should be particularly wary of the weak form *'d.* It is teachers who create the difficulty if, when meeting such a form, they ask *Is this short for 'should'* or *'would'?* A wrong answer will prompt a question of the difference between the two. It is safer and more constructive to teach particular uses, collect the uses of *one* of the forms, or, at higher levels, do major work over a period of time on the modal auxiliaries *as a group.*

The marginal modals

Native speakers are not completely consistent in their treatment of *should* and *would.* There are a number of other words semantically associated with the modal auxiliaries, where treatment is not consistent. It is not the intention of this book to present a comprehensive grammar of the English verb. My intention is to present the central, basic structure of the verb which is completely regular. This permits the identification of primary semantic characteristics and a complex of explanations covering almost all generative verb forms. The majority — the vast majority — of verb forms are covered by a remarkably simple, and totally consistent set of explanations. It would be surprising if something as complex as language was completely regular. It is clear that in the case of the modal auxiliaries there are marginal cases. These are *ought to, (have) to, need,* and *dare.*

Ought to

Both of the following may be used by native speakers:

You didn't ought to do that.
You oughtn't to do that.

In the second, *ought to* is treated as operator (it takes *n't*) while in the first case it is not.
The majority of British native speakers do treat *ought to* as an operator:

Ought we to let them know?
You ought not to ask.

It is clear that *ought to* shares semantic characteristics with the modal auxiliaries, in particular with *should.* The difference between these becomes clear if we contrast:

You ought not to do that.
I don't think you ought to do that.
You shouldn't do that.

The distinction resembles that between *(have) to* and *must. Must* is associated with the speaker's subjective perception of necessity, while *(have) to* is associated with external, objective necessity. The modal auxiliary *should* is associated with the speaker's perception of what is desirable; *ought to* is associated with what is externally, objectively, desirable. For this reason it carries connotations of right and wrong, of abstract desirability.

With this in mind it is easy to see why *I don't think you ought to do that* is closer in meaning to *You shouldn't do that* than to *You oughtn't to do that*. The sentence containing *should* involves the speaker's judgment through the modal auxiliary; when *ought to* is used, the speaker can introduce personal judgment through the use of a form such as *I think*.

(Have) to

We have already discussed these forms. There is not complete agreement among native speakers about the formal characteristics but there is a tendency not to treat *(have) to* as an operator. Although sentences like *Had you to show your ticket?* are acceptable, most native speakers probably prefer *Did you have to show your ticket?*

In a similar way, tags with *(have) to* tend to be made with *(do)* but not invariably:

You have to be careful these days, don't you?
I'm afraid they had to do it, hadn't they.

(Have) to and *ought to* are sometimes treated as operators, sometimes not. In contemporary English *ought to* is usually treated as an auxiliary and used as operator; usage with *(have) to* is more variable.

Semantically *(have) to* and *ought to* share an important characteristic — they are associated with objective rather than subjective perception of, respectively, necessity and desirability.

Occasionally *ought to* and *have to* can be combined:

They broke the fence down — they ought to have to fix it.

This sentence is about something as far from the speaker as the morality of the law, and contrasts strongly with *They should fix it* in which the speaker expresses a personal view about what should be done about the fence.

Need

Clearly, *need* is about necessity, and necessity is a modal concept. There are two forms in contemporary British English which it is easy to confuse. *Need to* is treated as a full verb:

Do I need to bring my own?
We don't need to pay, do we?

In a small number of items which are now almost lexical items or "linguistic fossils" *need* (without *to)* is still used as an operator:

Need I ask?
You needn't bring yours, you can borrow one from us.

From a classroom point of view it is certainly easier to treat *need to* as an ordinary verb, and introduce the operator (modal auxiliary) use of *need* as a lexical item.

Dare

This is extremely rare in contemporary English. In considering the basic structure of the English verb it could safely be ignored. There is certainly no justification for including it in the basic list of modal auxiliaries, where it will certainly cause unnecessary confusion.

Sometimes it is treated as a full verb, and, like *need to* it can be followed by *to:*

The water was so dirty we didn't dare to go swimming.
Nobody dared to say a word.

Very occasionally it is used as an operator, mostly in phrases which are now close to lexical items:

Dare I suggest we move on to the next item?

Swan, in *Practical English Usage,* describes a special case among the special cases:

> *I dare say* does not mean 'I dare to say'. It has almost the same meaning as 'probably' or 'I expect/ imagine/suppose'.
> It will rain tomorrow, I dare say.
> I dare say you're thirsty after all that tennis.

Once again it is clear that it is best to exclude *dare* from the basic list of modal auxiliaries, and treat those few phrases in which it remains possible as an operator as lexical items.

Summary

A basic list of modal auxiliaries can be identified:

can	**may**	**will**	**shall**	**must**
could	**might**	**would**	**should**	

Primary semantic characteristics can be identified for each of this basic list used as modal auxiliaries. The meanings are closely inter-related. Evidence of the coherence of the whole system is found in the close relationship between the pairs *will/shall, will/would, shall/should, should/would.*

Two areas of potential confusion are the other uses of *should,* and certain marginal modals. The coherence of that basic system is much clearer if these are dealt with as special cases.

15. The Passive; (be) + third form

All the verb forms we have considered so far are those traditionally called *active*. Within the verb phrase in statements the word order invariably is subject — verb; the statement tells us *who* did *what*. In certain situations, however, it is possible to express a different set of relationships, using the structure traditionally known as the *passive*. In English, it is characterised formally by *(be) + third form* of the verb. It may be combined with the other tense or aspect forms to produce complex forms. Here are some examples:

It was designed in Italy.
The road is being widened next year.
He had to be told.
We were caught on the wrong foot by the news.
It's taken from an original by Goya.

A small point of terminology may be noted. The traditional description of the form of the verb used to make the passive is the *past* participle. This is a source of some potential confusion as the form is also used to make *present* passive forms. This difficulty is overcome by adopting the simpler terminology *(be) + third form*.

Structurally the passive is simple. *Every* example of the passive is characterised by *(be) + third form*. Some traditional books, and even some published recently, make the *form* of the passive appear extremely complicated by presenting it in full paradigmatic form. Such a presentation is unnecessarily confusing. The present, past, and "perfect" passives can all be represented in the following simple table:

Present

I	'm	
he she it	's	asked
we you they	're	

Past

I he she it	was	
we you they	were	asked

Perfect

I you we they	have	been asked
he she it	has	

From *A Very Simple Grammar Of English, LTP, 1985*

The inevitable existence of a *(be)* auxiliary in passive forms means that the formation of questions, negatives, tags, interested responses etc. (See Chapter 7) is no more complex than with the verb *(be)* itself, or, for example, the "present continuous".

In forms which contain a passive and, a "perfect" or a "continuous" form, more than one auxiliary is involved, and that has sometimes led teachers to think that the passive is "difficult" from a structural point of view. The main difficulty is not structural, but semantic.

In language teaching the passive is nearly always presented as an *alternative* to the active. In most teaching, sentences such as:

Shakespeare wrote it.
→ It was written by Shakespeare.

are presented as "different ways of saying the same thing". It is true that the two sentences given have the same referential meaning, and that both are well-formed. It is not, however, true that for every well-formed passive sentence there is an underlying equivalent active sentence. Neither is it true that every active sentence may be turned into the passive. The central problem with the passive is to decide when it is appropriate or even necessary to use it. This question is usually completely avoided in language teaching.

Some dangers in the classroom

In any structural syllabus students meet active sentences before passive. The temptation, and general practice, is then to present the passive as a transformation of corresponding active sentences. Allsop says:

The general relationship between the ordinary (active) form and the passive form is:

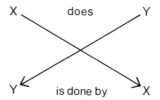

and this probably represents the most frequent way of introducing the passive.

The assumption is that the active is "ordinary", and the passive is in some way derived from it for special purposes. While it is true that the passive is sometimes used for stylistic reasons, in scientific writing for example, (see below) the passive is not a strange alternative for the active; it fulfils an essential role in the language and exists independently of the active.

If we begin from the position described by Allsop, we are then led into a discussion of the occasions on which the agent is omitted. Once more, the approach can *create* exceptions. It is simpler, and more logical to begin with examples where the "doer" of the action is unknowable:
The earth was formed millions of years ago.

By whom or by what is *unknowable,* or at the very least *unknown.* The passive will always be appropriate, and usually preferable, in cases where the doer is unknowable or unknown.

Sometimes, although the doer is unknown, both an active and a passive sentence, with the same referential meaning are possible:

My camera has been stolen.
Somebody has stolen my camera.

In this case, in order to produce an active sentence an artificial or dummy subject is introduced — *somebody*. It will be noted that here the active sentence presupposes "an unknown, but knowable person". If this presupposition is invalid, for example, because the natural presupposition is that the action was performed by a large number of nameless people, the passive will usually be preferred:

The whole town was rebuilt after the war.
At least five films of "Macbeth" have been made.

It is not easy to find natural active 'alternatives' for these examples.

It is true that in speech, and in informal writing, the active tends to be preferred to the passive, so that cases where "a general group" of people performed the action, *they* is frequently introduced as a "dummy subject":

The road is being widened.   → *They're widening the road.*
Taxes have been put up again. → *They've put up taxes again.*

The passive exists quite independently of the active. It is *obligatory* if the "doer" is unknowable. It is frequent, although optional, if the "doer" is a general group. It is possible, though less frequent if the "doer" is supposed by the speaker to be an unknown individual. If we develop this sequence — *unknowable, unknown,* one step further, we see that the passive will also be possible in certain cases where the "doer" is not of particular interest at the moment of speaking:

The house was sold again six months later.
Has your television been repaired yet?

Finally, the passive may be a pure stylistic variant. It is, for example, the standard in the describing of scientific experiments. It is considered "unscientific" to describe an experiment as follows, *I heated the test tube . . ,* the passive *The test tube was heated . . .* always being preferred. In this case it is the sense of objectivity given by the passive which causes the form to be preferred. The implication is clearly that if the reader repeats the experiment, the results will be the same; in other words, the "doer" was incidental to what was done.

Occasionally the passive is even more optionally a stylistic variant. For reasons of tact or modesty, for example, the passive or the use of a dummy subject, may be preferred to the "natural" active sentence in the following:

1a *An increase in the subscription was suggested.*
1b *Somebody suggested an increase in the subscription.*
1c *I suggested an increase in the subscription.*

2a *I was told you were leaving.*
2b *Somebody told me you were leaving.*
2c *Angela told me you were leaving.*

Much language teaching has misrepresented the passive. It has started by assuming it is a variation on the active. This is completely the wrong way round. The passive is necessary in certain cases of general, unknown agents. It is then generalisable to examples where, as the traditional explanation put it, "what is done is more important than who does it". The agent is only included in a passive sentence if it is essential to the meaning.

It is interesting to consider what certain discussions of the passive have to say on this matter.

Thomson and Martinet say the passive is used:

> When it is more convenient or interesting to stress the thing done than the doer of it, or when the doer is unknown: *My watch was stolen* is much more usual than *Thieves stole my watch.*

This is very little help. In the example given, *thieves* is little more than a substitute subject, a more concrete version of *somebody,* suggested by the semantics of *stolen.* The discussion (the only discussion of the use of the passive in the whole book) omits the essential information that it is the speaker who *chooses* a passive, and that in some cases a passive may be obligatory, or at least an active sentence highly unusual.

Allsop says:

> The subject of any sentence is the subject because it is what we are mainly interested in. . .To describe the use of the passive, we could begin this paragraph by saying:
> *We* use the passive to . . .
> The passive is used to . . .
> Because *the passive* in this case is more important than *we,* it would be logical to make the passive the subject of our sentence. In other words, the most important item becomes the subject of our sentence.

Again, there are two problems. In ". . . what *we* are mainly interested in", Allsop intends "we" to mean "the speaker". Throughout this book I have emphasised again and again that grammar is not only a matter of fact, but frequently a matter of the *speaker's* choice. The same point needs to be re-emphasised here.

Again, in the example given *we* is effectively a dummy subject. One of the ways of noting that the passive will be preferred, is to note that the natural active sentence suggested by the same referential meaning, will contain a dummy subject, often *they, we,* or *somebody.*

For the fullest discussion of the passive, the reader is referred to *Practical English Usage, paragraph 457.*

Swan's treatment, which is considerably fuller than any of the other works referred to, discusses the contrast between meaning and form, and the choice between active and passive constructions where these are optional. The area is complex, and Swan gives excellent guidance.

Some improbable forms

In theory, the passive can combine with all other verb forms; in practice, certain forms are very rare. The passive always involves *(be) + third form;* durative forms always *(be) + . . .ing.* Not surprisingly, passive duratives, containing *(be)* twice, are rare, although they do exist:

The road was being repaired last week.

Forms which contain *been being,* are even rarer: *He's been being treated with radium.*

As with certain other forms which are phonetically difficult, and consequently felt to be "ugly", these tend to be avoided.

Introducing the passive

It is not always clear if a sentence contains a passive. Some words have now passed into the language as adjectives:

I was late.
I was amazed.
I was amazed by what he said.

In the first sentence *late* is an adjective; in the second sentence it is perfectly possible to see *amazed* in the same way, as an adjective. It is also possible to see *was amazed* as a passive, and this tendency is slightly stronger in the last example where an "agent" is mentioned.

The reader may care to decide which of the following sentences contain adjectives, and which contain the passive:

Were you surprised?
They were attacked in the park.
I'm annoyed about that.
The shop was closed when I got there.
The road was closed by the police.
The music wasn't live — it was recorded.
Some of them are black and white and others are brightly coloured.

These few examples are sufficient to show that it is difficult to be decisive. If *open* in *The shop was open* is an adjective, it seems "logical" that *closed* in *The shop was closed* must also be an adjective. At the same time, it is easy to see *The road was closed by the police,* as an example of the passive.

Instead of seeing this as a source of confusion, however, we can see it as a source of help. Instead of introducing students to the passive through unnatural and contrived exercises of the "Make the following sentences passive. . ."kind, it may be much better pedagogically to introduce them to the passive through examples similar to the above, where the adjectival quality of the verb phrase leads students to an understanding of the use of the passive independently of the active.

It is also notable that the passive is usually taught relatively late in structural courses — it is seen as a "difficult" structure. In fact, it is no more difficult structurally than some of the sentences which will occur in the first few units of most course books.

A Are you French?   **A** Are you surprised?
B No I'm not, I'm German.   **B** No I'm not, I'm annoyed.

While I do not wish to recommend such artificial practices, it is useful to know that certain passives naturally occur quite independently of their "active equivalents", and that there is no justification for delaying the presentation of these important structures on grounds of difficulty.

Summary

Structurally, the passive is simple; all passive forms are marked by the occurrence of *(be) + third form*. This "factor" may be combined with others to form retrospective passives, durative passives etc. Certain forms, for stylistic or phonetic reasons, are unusual.

In general, the passive will be chosen if the doer of the action:

i.   is unknowable, or less restrictively,
ii. is an unknown general group, or, less restrictively,
iii. is unknown, or, less restrictively,
iv. is of less interest to the speaker in the particular context, than the action itself.

On most occasions, the "agent" (doer) is not mentioned. The agent is mentioned only if essential to the meaning.

16. Basic verb forms — A Summary

We have now completed our survey of all the basic structural features of the English verb. Almost all English verb forms may be generated, and their underlying meaning explained, by combining the primary semantic characteristics associated with each form. It is not possible to assert that the *whole* of the English verb can be reduced to a set of explanations which can be set out on a single page. On the other hand, neither is it true that the language is governed by "rules" riddled with "exceptions". There are a few cases, mostly "linguistic fossils", which are not generated by a combination of the following factors. The overwhelming majority of cases, however, are covered by this small number of grammatical features.

Two important features are made using operators, including the dummy auxiliary **(do):**

1. The positive verb phrase may be negated by the addition of *not (n't)* at the end of the first auxiliary:

2. The interrogative form may be made by inverting the order of the subject and first auxiliary.

English possesses two verb forms in which the speaker conceptualises a state, event or act as a fact. Fundamentally, the two forms represent different kinds of factuality, and do not necessarily suggest temporal interpretation.

3. The *basic form*, if used with a pronoun to form "the present simple", expresses immediate factuality. It is characteristic of the meaning of this form that the questions *When?* or *On what occasion?* are not appropriate. It does not express a fundamentally time-based conceptualisation.

4. The *remote form*, traditionally called "the past simple", is used when the speaker conceptualises an event factually, but as remote in some way. Most frequently this is remoteness in time, when the speaker refers in a non-interpretive way to a past event.

The other basic semantic features of the verb are characterised by particular elements in their form. Each structural element always contributes the same element to the meaning of the total form. Each of these forms is made using an auxiliary.

5. The speaker may draw particular attention to the fixed, or limited, duration of an event by using a form containing *(be)* + . . .*ing.* Such forms, frequently referred to as continuous or progressive, can usefully be referred to as *durative forms.*

6. The speaker can look back in time by using a form characterised by *(have)* + *third form*. The temporal interpretation of such forms means it is appropriate to refer to them as *retrospective* forms.

7. In a similar way the speaker can look forward using a *prospective* form, characterised by *(be) going to*.

8. The speaker can refer to an action without reference to an unknowable, unknown, or (at the moment of speaking) unimportant "doer", by using a *passive* form, characterised by *(be)* + *third form*.

9. The speaker may introduce an element of personal judgment of the non-temporal features of an action or event by using one of the *modal auxiliaries*. For each of these modal auxiliaries, primary semantic characteristics of a basic meaning can be identified.

Complex verb phrases are made by combining several of the factors listed above, in examples such as:

Could he have been trying to ring us?
It had been being built for two years already.

Certain forms are much more frequent than others. Some combinations are semantically impossible and do not occur. Some are phonologically difficult — for example, the second sentence given above containing both *been* and *being* — and are infrequent. Some longer verb phrases include factors which rarely co-occur — retrospection and prospection, for example, though they are possible:

He must have been going to tell her anyway.

In some cases there is "agreement" between the different parts; if the modal is removed from *He must have been waiting,* it becomes *He has been waiting.*

A few verb forms are not generated by the general characteristics just defined. Among these are the marginal modals, *used to,* and inversions with *should.* However, the vast majority of English verb forms are analysable as combinations of the factors listed. This means a form such as "the past continuous", may be explained not as an independent form, but as a *combination* of the remote and durative forms.

17. Future Time — A Summary

English possesses no formal future tense but, of course, it is possible to talk about Future Time. A number of different verb forms are possible and the choice of the correct one is frequently a source of confusion for foreign learners. It is not posssible to give simple, easily accessible, comprehensive rules which describe the differences between the different possible forms. Much of the discussion in this book has concentrated upon the fact that verb forms are frequently a matter of the speaker's choice. This applies particularly to events in Future Time which are not, of their nature, factually or objectively knowable in the same way that events in Past Time or Present Time are.

Examination of the uses of those verb forms which sometimes refer to Future Time and sometimes do not, shows that *all* uses of the form always have the same primary semantic characterisitics. Those occasions when the verb form is used with reference to Future Time are not different in kind. The consistency and regularity of the use of the verb forms which is one of the central themes of this book are fully preserved.

In several cases, uses of the forms which refer to Future Time are discussed in the appropriate chapters. Some of the contrasts are gathered together here for convenience. Six verb forms are common to refer to Future Time:

(1) I'm going to leave tomorrow.
(2) I'm leaving tomorrow.
(3) I leave tomorrow.
(4) I am to leave tomorrow.
(5) I'll leave tomorrow.
(6) I'll be leaving tomorrow.

Statements about Future Time are not statements of fact but predictions, guesses, etc. We expect the different forms chosen in some way to reflect the differing nature of the guesses, predictions, etc. Examination of how the forms are used, shows that they are used consistently and that the choices depend on how the speaker conceptualises the future event at the moment of speaking. It is helpful in considering the speaker's conceptualisation to ask *why* the speaker thinks the future event will occur.

Not "degree of certainty"

Some readers may be familiar with the suggestion made by Leech (*Meaning and the English Verb, Longman, 1971*) that the choice of verb appropriate for a future event may be decided according to the degree of certainty ascribed to the future happening. He suggests:

(1) Simple present (most certain)

(2) $\begin{cases} \text{will/shall + infinitive} \\ \text{will/shall + progressive infinitive} \end{cases}$

(3) $\begin{cases} \text{be going to + infinitive} \\ \text{present progressive} \end{cases}$ (least certain)

Even those marked "least certain", however, convey at least a strong expectation of the future event.

Such an explanation is attractive because it is fairly simple for both teacher and student to grasp. There are, however, two difficulties — firstly, if the explanation is true, the difference between the various degrees of certainty is extremely subtle and, however simple the explanation is in theory, it is of little practical use. Secondly, however, there is a much greater problem — it is, quite simply, that the explanation is not true. I have on numerous occasions when speaking to native speaker audiences asked them to rate in order of "degree of certainty" the sentences given at the beginning of the chapter. On every single occasion when I have done this with an audience of more than 12 the voting for "most certain" and "least certain" has split over at least three of the examples. Not infrequently some native speakers have voted one example "most certain" while others in the same group have voted the same example "least certain". If native speakers cannot even agree on which is most or least certain, they are going to find it impossible to range the other examples between the two extremes. Such evidence seems to me to prove conclusively that "degree of certainty" is not only an impractical classroom explanation, it is also completely without foundation.

The essential distinction between the different forms is the nature of the speaker's conceptualisation of the future act or event. Nobody except the speaker can *know* the speaker's conceptualisation. All we can do, is to point to parallels with other uses of the same form, or contrasts with the uses of different forms, to indicate the nature of the events described by particular verb forms.

1. (be) going to

This form is used if, at the moment of speaking, the speaker has *evidence* for the future event. That evidence may be either external (clouds or a tickle in the nose) or internal (a plan or decision):

It's going to rain.
I'm going to sneeze.
I'm not going to tell you.

From the speaker's point of view such uses are similar; in each case the evidence is clear to the speaker, and the future act is seen as the culmination of a previous sequence of events or thoughts. The future event is a projection or extrapolation of events preceding, and up to, the point Now.

Statements of the "internal evidence" type, will frequently begin with "I"; questions using this form more frequently involve "you" or a third person:

I'm definitely not going to take the exam in summer.
Are you going to take the exam this summer?
Is he going to go to university?

Other combinations can occur:

What on earth am I going to do about it?
You are definitely not going to borrow mine!

but of course *my* internal evidence tends to be about me and *questions* about internal evidence are usually about other people.

(be) going to is non-modal. It does not involve the speaker's personal judgment and, in particular, is non-volitional. Events described using *(be) going to* are seen as arising out of a process which is already in progress at the time of speaking. This is clear from an example such as:

What do you think is going to happen next?

where the listener's opinion is sought about something which happens independently of speaker or listener.

In some ways *(be) going to* forms are similar to *(be)* + . . .*ing* forms. There is, however, one important distinction.

2. The present durative

It is not always possible to use the present durative to refer to Future Time:

(1)   **It's raining tomorrow.*
(2)   *I'm playing tennis on Saturday.*
(3)   **(?) I'm watching TV tomorrow evening.*

Example (1) is impossible; (2) seems natural and (3), although possible, is less likely than an alternative form, e.g. *I'm going to watch* . . . or *I'll be watching* . . . .

We need to think once more of the defining characteristics of the present durative. It is used if, at the moment of speaking, the speaker conceptualises the action as occurring between precisely two points in time, one before and one after the point Now. At the moment of speaking the speaker has in mind two points, one on either side of Now, between which the action, as far as the speaker is concerned, exists. It can be represented diagrammatically:

We see immediately why (1) is impossible. There is no way that the speaker can have in mind at Now some event which pre-dates Now and which is conceptualised as an intrinsic part of *It's raining tomorrow.* This contrasts with *I'm seeing him tomorrow* in which the arrangement of the meeting pre-dates Now and is seen by the speaker as an intrinsic part of the future act.

It is easy to see why *arrangements,* particularly made between the speaker and another person, may be expressed using this form. The speaker has in mind a precise event which pre-dates Now — the making of the arrangement — and an event which post-dates Now — the performing of the action itself, and, seeing these two events as linked and surrounding Now, chooses the verb form which expresses exactly those characteristics.

In example (2), we know that tennis involves playing with other people and that, therefore, some event must have preceded Now for the speaker to be able to make the statement about tomorrow. For this reason example (2) seems natural.

Example (3) feels a little unnatural; television watching is not usually arranged but, equally, on exactly those occasions when there is an event which pre-dates the moment of speaking and culminates in the performance of the action, example (3) will be appropriate.

The use of the present continuous to refer to Future Time is by no means random. The meaning of the *(be)* + ...*ing* form interacts with the meaning of the verb itself. In some cases the combination is semantically impossible with Future Time reference, in others frequent, and in others rare. The form is used for precisely the same reasons to refer to Future Time as for all other uses. The frequently-used heading "the present continuous used for the future" is an illusion; such uses are exactly like all others.

"Yes, Charlie—I'm pretty sure she's giving me a cordless telephone."

A pair such as :

What will you do when you leave school?
What are you doing when you leave school?

are both possible but suggest very different situations. The first suggests the speaker is inviting the other person to discuss the question and that the listener's present opinion is of immediate interest; the second suggests that the speaker would like to know the arrangements which the other person has already made, or thoughts he has already had; it is more a request for information.

As we have seen on several occasions in this book when considering contrasting pairs of this kind, the connotational differences understood by the hearer are a direct result of the meanings characteristically associated with the verb forms chosen.

The inclusion of *will* or *'ll,* being modal, concentrates on the precise moment of speaking, Now; the present durative associates the future event with a point which precedes Now.

The present durative with reference to Future Time resembles *(be) going to,* in that both relate the event in Future Time to something preceding Now. The distinction, sometimes slight, is that with the present durative there is usually a single event which pre-dates Now, whereas with *(be) going to* there is a sequence of events up to Now which the speaker projects forward to the future event. The contrast is clear with the pair:

What are you doing tomorrow?   *What are you going to do tomorrow?*

The first asks about the event you have already planned, and which will occur tomorrow; the second enquires about the listener's thinking *up to now* about tomorrow. With the present durative the event which pre-dates Now is more isolated from Now; with *(be) going to* there is something which pre-dates Now, but what is happening *at* the moment of speaking is also important.

3. The "present simple"

The basic form is used when the lexical meaning of the verb alone is sufficient to convey the full message. With a pronoun, in "the present simple", it is used when the speaker conceptualises the event as "pure fact". It is associated with "simple facts", objective truth. Time reference is accidental to the occurrence of this form; it is appropriate precisely on the occasions that the questions *When?* and *On what occasion ?* are not appropriate. (This was discussed in detail in Chapter 8.)

The form will be appropriate for events in Future Time when the speaker sees the future event as occurring quite independently of his understanding, perception, volition, etc. The event is determined by what the speaker sees as an external *force majeure*. This may be natural, or an appropriate timetable – making body:

Christmas day falls on a Thursday this year.
What time does the sun rise next Saturday?
Arsenal play away next weekend.
We leave at 4 o'clock tomorrow afternoon.

It is comparatively unusual for this form to be used about *I* or *we* and notice that, in the example just given which contains *we,* the suggestion is clearly that we are catching a train or coach, rather than that we will be setting off with our own car, in which case *We're leaving about 4 tomorrow* or *We are going to leave at 4 tomorrow* would be more natural.

As we saw in Chapter 8 the verb form in: *We leave at 4 o'clock* is not intrinsically associated with a particular point in time. The occurrence of the phrase *at 4 o'clock* is coincidental, and not intrinsic to the choice of the form *leave.*

We have seen that the speaker can express a temporal view of the action by using the *(be) + . . .ing* or *(be) going to* forms. If such marked forms are inappropriate, the speaker selects the basic form. In the case of Future Time reference, when the event is in no way dependent upon the speaker, the basic form is appropriate. Such uses are relatively rare, but entirely consistent with all other uses of this form.

4. (be) to

We have not considered this form elsewhere in this book. It is relatively rare in spoken English, but occurs in newspapers, and some relatively formal writing. Here are some examples:

The work is to be completed by the end of June.
The Queen is to visit Canada in October.
There's to be an enquiry into the whole affair.

The form *(be) to* also occurs in the remote form:

At that time he did not know he was to be king.
That wasn't the end of it — worse was to follow.

Uses referring to Past Time provide an insight into the semantic characteristics of the form. *Worse followed* describes the event factually, and, from the speaker's point of view, as a remote fact. It is not, however, possible to make a similar transformation of the first sentence: *At that time he did not know that he was king.*

(be) to describes events which the speaker sees as facts, but as *future* facts, rather than pure, timeless facts, expressed, as always through the basic form.

With *was/were to,* in Past Time the events are seen as pure facts. They can, however, be described as future facts, from a point of view in the past. This is exactly the case with *At that time. . .* in the example. The introductory adverbial, placing the speaker's temporal point of view decisively at a point in Past Time, means a *(be) to* form is required by the meaning. With the example *Worse followed,* or *Worse was to follow* the difference, though less obvious, is the same; *followed* states the remote factuality of what happened for the speaker now; *was to follow* describes the past event factually, from a point of view in Past Time.

The same considerations apply to "present" uses of *(be) to.* Like the basic form, the event is described as *fact.* The distinction is made between future fact — *(be) to* and "timeless" fact — the basic form. Not surprisingly, both forms are relatively rare and the difference between them often small.

Consideration of most "present" uses of *(be) to,* however, reveals that the certainty about the future event is nearly always based on a formal announcement made by some authority which, through experience, is seen as irrevocable, and therefore certain. Events described by *(be) to* are nearly always based on an announcement of a single, particular event. The basic form is more frequent if the same impersonal *force majeure* is involved, but based on more regular, general and therefore timeless, information.

We are to leave at 4 suggests a guide or driver has just told me about a *particular* departure. *We leave at four this afternoon,* although apparently "a future fact", is much more likely to be a reference to the *normal* timetable.

The basic form and *(be) to* share a sense of factuality. They differ in that the basic form is associated with timeless factuality, while *(be) to* is associated with future factuality. Because future factuality is unusual, *(be) to* forms are rare.

The similarity of *(be) to* and *(have) to*

We noted that *(have) to* is not a modal auxiliary; it is about abstract, objective necessity. *(be) to* is similar; it is about abstract, objective future factuality. It is the English "future as fact".

Its authority and force are clear in a relatively unusual example such as *You are to be there by 3 o'clock.* The meaning is close to *You have to be . . .* Both suggest external reasons, rather than a personal suggestion of the speaker.

This example also parallels closely an example with Past Time reference discussed above:

At that time, he did not know he was to be king.	*You are to be there by 3 o'clock.*
*At that time, he did not know he was king.	**You are there at 3 o'clock.*

(be) to expresses pure factual futurity, or future factuality.

Newspaper headlines

Newspaper headlines provide evidence for the analysis just discussed. Here are three examples:

1. **GOVERNMENT ANNOUNCES TAX REDUCTIONS** 2. **QUEEN TO VISIT CHINA** 3. **UNEMPLOYMENT FALLING**

1. It will be noted that the basic form ("present simple") is used for an event which lies in Past Time, but which is conceptualised as an undivided whole, and the subject of *immediate* interest.

2. The general convention of headlines is that *(be)* auxiliaries are frequently omitted. It is therefore not at all surprising that *to* denotes future fact, as discussed in *(be) to* above.

3. Similarly, events surrounding Now are usually headlined with a . . .*ing* form, as we might expect from consideration of *(be)* + . . .*ing* forms.

5. will/shall/'ll

We have noted that the essential characteristic of forms containing *will/shall/'ll* is that they are modal. This means they are essentially grounded in the moment of speaking. They express ideas which may be paraphrased as "given the circumstances I see at the moment, I consider it is . . . that. . . .".

Both *will* and *shall* express the idea of the inevitable connection between two states, one pertaining at the moment of speaking and a second state. If the inevitable connection is a connection in time, *will* and *shall* refer to Future Time. The expression of Future Time with *will* and *shall* differs from the forms discussed above in its concentration upon the moment of speaking, Now, and in the speaker's involvement.

With two of the forms we have considered, the speaker sees the event factually. With the two others which include aspectual forms, the speaker interprets future events with reference to purely temporal characteristics. In both the present durative and *(be) going to* forms, the speaker sees something which pre-dates Now as a reason for the future event. In future forms involving a modal, the emphasis is on the speaker's judgment at the moment of speaking. The reader is referred to pages 117 to 119 for further discussion of *will/shall* with reference to Future Time.

Speculation

If most native speakers are asked for the future of *I hit him,* they suggest *I'll hit him.* There is a tendency even for native speakers to believe that *'ll* is "the future" in English. We have seen that this is not technically true; it is not possible to identify the expression of Future Time with *will/shall/'ll,* nor *will/shall/'ll* with the expression of Future Time. Nonetheless, it is clear that the unstressed form, *'ll,* expressing as it does a concept of weak inevitability and psychological immediacy, must approximate to "a neutral future". It is interesting to speculate that the *'ll* form is evolving in the direction of a neutral future — an English "future tense". This view is partially supported by the evidence of *The Daily Telegraph* birthday announcements. Each day the birthdays of prominent people are announced. The normal form for such announcements is: *Miss Brigitte Bardot is 51 today.* On Saturdays, (the paper is not published on Sundays) they do, however, also include: *Mr. Trevor Howard will be 69 tomorrow.*

It is possible to say *I'm 35 on Saturday,* or *I'll be 35 on Saturday.* The newspaper, however, exhibits a clear tendency to treat *will be* as appropriate for Future Time.

18. Some areas of misunderstanding

(1) "Short forms"

As a matter of convention, in written English only the full forms of auxiliaries are used (other than, for example, in personal letters which, for this purpose, may be characterised as "written spoken English" rather than written English). Textbooks are, by their very nature written. Most modern methodologies have, however, for many years, encouraged students to say sentences of the target language from an early stage. Such speaking has frequently been supported by printed text. Confusion has, perhaps inevitably, resulted.

Many teachers, teacher trainers and textbook writers have worried about the methodological question of whether to present students with the full printed forms first, or the natural reduced spoken forms. This methodological question has, unfortunately, obscured a more fundamental question and encouraged a serious misunderstanding.

In writing, other than the informal writing of personal letters referred to above, only one form, the full form, is used.

In speech both the full and reduced forms of the auxiliary †are common. It is possible, and natural, to say both of:

I've been waiting 20 minutes.　　*That was kind of you.*
I have been waiting 20 minutes.　　*That **was** kind of you.*

As we see, in some cases, there is a convention for writing "the short form", in others not. In all cases, however, two clearly distinguishable forms exist in speech. Those two different forms, following the Principle of General Use discussed in Chapter 3, have different meanings.

Teachers will make an immediate improvement if they avoid equating "the short form" with "the spoken form". They will, however, also need to teach the difference between the stressed and weak forms in speech. Some occurrences of the weak or strong form are determined by phonological considerations:

A Are you German?　　**A** Are you French?
B Yes, I am.　　　　　**B** No, I'm not.

The stressed form is used in the positive response because the *am* is at the end, while the weak form is used in the negative response, because in this case the heavy stress falls on *not*. It is also possible, however, to respond naturally *No, I am not.* This is not synonymous with *No I'm not.*

In general, weak forms are used in speech if the speaker intends no particular emotional force to attach to the expression. If particular emotional force is intended, the auxiliary is stressed.

† Parts of the verbs *(have)* and *(be)* behave similarly even when they occur as full verbs.

The importance of the stress on the auxiliary is that the speaker intends particular emotional force to be attached to the expression. In particular contexts, looked at from a communicative point of view, it will be possible to identify the reasons for the emotional force, for example, enthusiasm, annoyance, insistence, etc.

These observations while not profound, have considerable implications for teaching methodology and for the content of what is taught. The methodological argument over which of the spoken and written forms should be presented first is a red herring, based on a false contrast. The important information students need is:

(i) In all except private letters auxiliaries are written in full. (There are other technical occasions on which this is not true — when a dramatic writer is attempting to simulate speech or, like a linguist, is transcribing speech. Then forms such as *You'd've been very surprised* need to be used).

(ii) The auxiliary in English is either reduced, or stressed. The connotational meanings of the reduced and stressed forms are different.

(iii) Communicatively, the student needs to learn how to express particular functions e.g. expressing annoyance, through use of a stressed auxiliary: *I have been waiting 20 minutes; I did remind you.*

Students must be discouraged from producing a neutral auxiliary. Not only is it important for them to *understand* the difference between the stressed and unstressed forms, they need to be encouraged, from the earliest stages of learning to hear and to produce both stressed and weak forms. Simple listening practices *("Which word in what the speaker says has the heaviest stress?")* and simple productive practices *("Say these sentences, first with a weak auxiliary, secondly with a stressed auxiliary")* are important.

Stress is an important feature of the *grammar* of a language. It is a mistake to believe that students can be taught structure and will 'acquire' stress with no teaching. If it is worth drawing students' attention to structural patterns, it is equally important to draw their attention to stress patterns.

(2) Conditional Sentences

It is the verb phrase not the sentence which is the fundamental unit requiring analysis. Certain combinations are, for semantic reasons, highly frequent, while others are less frequent or even impossible.

A particular misunderstanding frequently arises in the teaching of so-called conditional sentences. It is common to teach three "basic" kinds:

(1) *If he comes I'll ask him.*
(2) *If he came I'd ask him.*
(3) *If he'd come I would've asked him.*

These are frequently referred to as:

(1) The first conditional, or *likely* conditions.
(2) The second conditional, or *unlikely* conditions.
(3) The third conditional, or *impossible* conditions.

The three examples given are all well-formed sentences of types which would be relatively frequent in much written English. Readers may care, however, to examine the following list and mark the sentences which they consider to be well-formed:

1. If he would come, I'd ask him.
2. If he'll come, I'll ask him.
3. If he's come, I'll ask him.
4. If he's going to come, I'd ask him.
5. If he could come, I'd ask him.
6. If he can come, I'll ask him.
7. If he might come, I'd ask him.
8. If he comes, I'm going to ask him.
9. If we hadn't been going to ask him, he wouldn't have been invited.
10. If he hadn't been invited by us, he wasn't going to get an invitation at all.

In fact *all* of these examples are well-formed English sentences. If students are taught *only* the first, second and third conditionals, they will know only a small, admittedly highly frequent, sub-set of the possibilities. It is not necessary to teach the fourth conditional, the fifth conditional, etc., but it is important to recognise that the possibility arises from the *meaning* of the individual clauses and that there are many more possibilites than those frequently presented in language teaching textbooks. The explanation of the use of a form in a conditional sentence is exactly the same as that of its occurrence in any other utterance. The underlying principle behind this is that each main verb phrase is treated independently.

An understanding of the importance of the verb phrase rather than the sentence has two important practical consequences, one at lower levels and one for more advanced students.

As soon as we turn our attention to the spoken language we note that interchanges such as the following are common:

A *Are we going to ask him?*
B *If we have to.*

A *Are you going to bring your car?*
B *If it would help.*

A *Are you going on Saturday?*
B *If it doesn't rain.*

In traditional structuralist courses " the conditional" is taught at a relatively late stage. In a communicative syllabus this is most unsatisfactory — it is by no means true that because one is a comparative beginner one only wishes to make unqualified remarks. The teaching of "the conditional" as if it were a special form is theoretically unsound. There is no reason at all why expressions introduced by *if* or *unless* cannot be introduced into a course at a comparatively early stage. This increases the student's communicative ability, and provides an introduction to the more complex conditional structures which are comparatively common in the written language.

Teachers should also note that introducing *would* as "the English conditional" is extremely, and unnecessarily, confusing. *Would* frequently occurs in conditional sentences but, as we have seen with the Principle of General Use, it is important to avoid teaching a partial truth as a generally applicable rule. The following are in no sense 'conditional':

Would you like a cup of tea?
It would take about three days.

It is not uncommon to argue that such sentences contain a "covert" condition but, if that is the case, so does: *I'm taking my umbrella (even if it isn't raining yet).*

Incidentally, like many conditional clauses in English, this clause does not contain *would* — further evidence that *would* is *not* "the conditional" in English. English simply does not have "a conditional tense". These difficulties are avoided quite simply if *would* is treated as a modal auxiliary, and not referred to as "the conditional". With modern functional methodology this is not a very radical suggestion. It is clear that expressions such as *Would you like a cup of tea?* are best explained as "when you want to offer somebody something, or invite them to do something, use *Would you like . . .* or *Would you like to . . .*". The functional description is a sufficient explanation of the meaning *and* use of the form. It is confusing and unnecessry to dissect its structural characteristics.

For many school students the main problem with conditionals is one of manipulating the various auxiliaries which occur. Most mistakes are mistakes of form. This suggests that school students do require practice of the forms of such highly occurrent uses as the so-called first, second and third conditionals.

At higher levels, however, students are frequently inhibited from forming natural expressions of their own because of the restrictive rules with which they have been presented. For such students it would be helpful to present them with a large list similar to that presented above and invite them to:
(a) divide the list into those forms which are possible and those which are not
(b) discuss together the *possible* patterns.
The truth towards which they should be led is that the possibilities in conditionals are identical to those in "non-conditional" uses.

(3) Tags

The terminal phrases in:

It's a lovely day, isn't it.
I don't think you're allowed to smoke in here, are you?

are an important feature of spoken English. In common with many other features of the spoken, rather than written, language they have been widely misunderstood. Again we note that difference of form implies difference of meaning. The 'surface' difference may be structural or involve stress or intonation. The area of misunderstanding is immediately highlighted if we consider the words:

she's married isn't she

This may be said in (at least) two clearly distinct ways:

(1) *She's married, isn't she?*
(2) *She's married isn't she.*

In the first case the speaker believes she is married and seeks confirmation of the fact. The speaker does not *know* for certain and does, therefore, require some information. Such tag usages may reasonably be referred to as *question tags*. They are marked by a particular pattern of pause and intonation. (And in this chapter only tags of this kind are marked by a comma and question mark indicating these spoken features).

Although containing "exactly the same words", (2) is quite distinct. Said with a falling intonation, and probably with less of a pause "before the tag", it does not seek an "informational" answer in the way that (1) does. If the characteristic of a *question* is that it seeks information, this is not, in that sense, a question. The difference of stress and intonation implies a difference of meaning. Examples (1) and (2) are communicatively quite distinct. Because of the structural nature of many traditional grammar books, and much textbook presentation, it is, however, usual to teach all of these under the single heading "question tags". As the example above shows, this is an important misunderstanding.

The difference between the two uses is immediately apparent if we consider *It's a lovely day isn't it.* It is easy to imagine situations in which this could be said following the pattern of example (2), but very difficult to conceive of a situation where pattern (1) would be appropriate. If two people meet it is almost inconceivable that one will "suspect" that it is a nice day, and wish to confirm the fact with the other (unless, for example, one is confined by illness to a room with closed curtains or some similar situation).

It is also clear that there is a mis-match between the speaker's expectations and the responses in the following:

A *It's a lovely morning isn't it.*
B *Yes.*
A *It looks as if you'll be able to go to the beach doesn't it.*
B *Yes.*
A *You're quite a good swimmer aren't you.*
B *Yes.*

Whatever intonation patterns are used here, B is either very annoyed or exceptionally difficult to talk to. The importance of this example is that, if the tags are indeed questions, B has "answered" each question and the source of the misunderstanding is a mystery. The example shows clearly that "grammar" includes structure, stress and intonation. Concentration upon structure alone is a dangerous misunderstanding.

We can identify two important, and distinct, uses of tags:

(1) *She's married, isn't she?* Said in a particular way this means the speaker suspects or assumes the truth from the main sentence and asks the hearer to confirm it. The appropriate response would be to answer the question. We may reasonably call these *question tags*.

(2) *She's married isn't she.* Said with falling intonation, this invites the hearer to comment on the subject matter of the main sentence, *and to add new information* to extend the conversation. It is not a "question" which seeks an informational aswer, but an invitation to conversation. The appropriate response will usually contain a form of "dummy answer" (see below) *and* new information or an opinion. We may call these *invitation (or comment) tags*.

The structural rules for both kinds of tag are identical and may be summarised as:
Positive sentence — Negative tag
Negative sentence — Positive tag
The tag contains the first auxiliary of the appropriate verb phrase; if there is no auxiliary the pattern is preserved by using *(do)* as dummy auxiliary (see

Chapter 7).

The normal expected response to an invitation tag has two parts — a "dummy answer", frequently consisting of *Yes/No* and the formal manipulation of the auxiliary, followed by additional new information or an opinion:

A *You know David Brown don't you.*
B *Yes I do. We used to work together.*

A *You can't speak Spanish can you.*
B *No I can't. I went to classes a couple of years ago but I didn't get very far.*

It will be noted that the first part of these responses — the "dummy answer" is structurally identical with the answer to the corresponding question tag. Communicatively it is important to recognise that invitation tags also anticipate an original contribution given in the second part of each of B's responses above. Simple "answers" usually indicate an unwillingness to talk, and therefore some negative attitude such as hostility, annoyance or indifference to the other person.

There are several other less common varieties of tags, the use and structure of which are clearly distinct from those already described. Perhaps the most common of these is:

Oh, you've met before, have you!
Oh, you should, should you!
Oh, he wasn't, wasn't he!
Oh, he knew, did he!

In these examples positive sentences have positive tags, and negative sentences have negative tags. Tags of this kind, of which even many advanced students are unaware, are normally used to express surprise or annoyance.

There are also certain tags which cannot be predicted from the descriptive rules given so far which are used with specific meanings:

Pass the salt, will you.
Pass the salt, would you.

These may be used as alternatives to *please* (to family or close friends).

Let's go to the cinema, shall we.

This resembles invitation tags in that it invites a response rather than an answer, but is structurally unlike any of the tags referred to so far, and needs to be learned as a special case.

Tags are an important feature of the informal conversation of British native speakers. Any communicative methodology will need to give them more priority than would be the case in a purely structural course.

Structurally they are an important feature, depending as they do upon the flexibility of the English auxiliaries and the dummy auxiliary *(do)*.

There is good reason to introduce them into normal school classes — they provide effective practice of an important structural feature of the language, and are of importance in natural communication. They can be introduced in highly traditional drill format, both with the objective of encouraging greater facility in manipulating the auxiliaries (including the dummy) and of ensuring that such structures as:

It isn't quite right, is it.
It couldn't be this one, could it?
Yes it is, isn't it.

begin to sound and feel natural in the ears and mouths of students.

For many schoolteachers their students will meet only question and invitation tags. Students will need extensive practice in formulating natural responses, particularly to invitation tags.

In order to avoid confusion for those students who meet other tags at a later stage — for example, the surprise/annoyance tags referred to above — it is helpful if teachers regularly refer to *question tags* and *invitation tags* rather than using the general word *tags,* or using the general, traditional "question tags". The structural and intonational rules for forming question and invitation tags are quite different from those used for forming other kinds of tag. If teachers choose terminology carefully, there is less chance of confusion for those who go on to more advanced English studies.

Summary

The three points discussed in this chapter are frequently misunderstood and a source of confusion. It is worth noting that the problems have something in common. Two are based on ignoring features of the spoken language — stress and intonation — and concentrating on the appearance of the language on a page. Curiously, the problem of conditionals is similar — it arises from placing too great an emphasis on the sentence, failing to recognise the verb phrase as the most important feature. Simple and naturally occurring "conditions" *(If it rains)* are ignored at the expense of the forms which are common in the written language.

It seems to me there is a general, and important, point here. Contrary to popular belief, the spoken language is frequently *more* regular than the written language. The written language is beset by many conventions ("rules") which, while claiming to standardise, frequently give artificial preference to one form over another and thereby introduce irregularity. One extremely obvious observation should constantly be in teachers' minds — nobody writes a language well, which he does not first speak well. In contrast, it is possible to speak fluently and well, without having great mastery of the written forms. This applies even to a person's native language — writing well is a minority skill. If school students are to learn a foreign language well, it is essential to maintain high motivation and enjoyment. This is done partly by placing great emphasis on oral skills at the expense of written skills. This needs to continue for a long time — perhaps even through the whole of the student's school career. I believe this is not only methodologically a good idea, it is also totally theoretically sound and will lead also to a greater insight into, and ability to use, the foreign language in *all* its forms.

19. Some additional problems

This book does not pretend to be a comprehensive grammar of the English verb. My object is to show that there is a huge central, and totally regular system to the English verb which covers the great majority of examples. It is not true that English is totally regular — even in the central area discussed in this book, we have noted marginal cases and verb forms which are treated in different ways by native speakers. In addition, there are a number of forms which have not been discussed at all. Some of these are a source of confusion but they have been excluded because they are not part of the basic, generalisable and generative structure of the English verb. Some of them are mentioned briefly here.

1. Subjunctive

The *University Grammar of English* lists three kinds of subjunctive:

a. the "mandative" subjunctive in *that*-clauses: *It was/is necessary that every member inform himself of these rules.*
b. Lexical items which need to be learned as whole expressions.
c. *If I were . . . .*

The first case is extremely rare, and indeed not used by a large number of native speakers. It is almost certainly disappearing from the language. While a comprehensive grammar will need to include it, it is difficult to justify including it in any grammar for foreign students, unless they are studying linguistics or the history of English.

The lexical items are best treated as such — presented as fixed expressions which can be learned. Examples include *God save the Queen* (which is minimally generative: *God bless you, God grant you mercy) May you live long and die happy.*

Although *If I were . . .* is minimally generative, it too is probably best treated as a lexical item. In almost all sentences other than *If I ...*, the vast majority of native speakers now prefer, for example, *If he was here, he'd tell you himself.*

In short, the few linguistic fossils which constitute "the English subjunctive", can be dealt with as lexical items. They in no way contribute to an understanding of the basic structure of the contemporary English verb. Is not a term schoolchildren learning English should ever meet!

(have) + got

There is an extremely complex and "messy" area of usage in which *(have)* may occur alone, or in combination with *(get)*.

They have three children.	*They've got three children.*
I have to be there by 3 o'clock.	*I've got to be there by 3 o'clock.*

The difficulty covers both *(have)* and *(have) to*.

In general throughout this book I have suggested that difference of form implies difference of meaning. I have to confess that with some of the *(have)* v *(have) got* contrasts, I can distinguish no consistent patterns of semantic distinction. The choice frequently seems to be idiolectal, or decided by such arbitrary rules-of-thumb as "You should never write *got*".

Teachers and students will of course meet examples of combinations with *(got)*, and some remarks about more or less likely forms can be made but definite rules cannot be given and combinations with *(got)* do not form part of the basic, generative structure of the English verb.

Teachers may find the following comments helpful in the classroom, but these are in no sense comparable to the other rules discussed in this book;

(have) is not normally used to talk about possession; *(have) got* is normally used: *Have you got any money with you?*

Had alone is usually preferred to *had got* in the past: *I had an old Ford before I bought the Volvo.*

Had to is usually preferred to *had got to* in the past: *We had to catch the early train.*

The imperative

Let's is sometimes presented as part of the "imperative". It is not, and again is best treated as a lexical item defined by its function:

Let's stop for a break, shall we. (note the tag)

Note also that both negatives are found:
Let's not say anything at the moment.
Don't let's say anything at the moment.

It is sometimes argued that the "negative imperative" is *Don't*. This is unhelpful. In fact, once again there is a regularity in the verb which is frequently overlooked.

The basic form may be used if the whole message is conveyed by the lexical meaning of the verb: *Push, Tear to open.*

It is frequently forgotten that invitations, warnings, or expressions of irritation can be made with *Do:*

Do help yourselves!	*Do take care!*	*Do pay attention!*

As in all other uses of the dummy auxiliary, *n't* may be added:

Don't wait for me	*Don't be late.*	*Don't do that!*

If English does have an imperative, it must be *Do. . .*, but this way of looking at things is unnecessarily complicated when this verb form can easily be presented functionally.

Would

In the chapter on modal auxiliaries we saw that the modal auxiliary *would* has a single definable meaning. We ignored expressions such as:

Would that I could!   *Would that I had!*

Again, expressions with *Would that ...* are rare, and at an appropriately advanced level can be presented as lexical items, rather than a structural feature.

"The future"

We have discussed six verb forms which are frequently used to refer to Future Time. We have ignored others, such as *(be) about to:*

I'm just about to have my dinner.   *I was about to ring you.*

Such forms have not been considered only because they do not have the generative power of the basic factors which have been discussed.

Some classroom problems

The primary concern of this book is to establish the meaning of the individual verb forms in English. Attention is centred upon the language itself, and upon the semantics of the forms. Teachers will not need to be told that a number of language features which cause considerable problems in the classroom, have not been discussed. The three most obvious are the third person-**s**, the exception to the general negative rule, *will + not = won't,* and the practical classroom problem caused by the difference between verbs containing an auxiliary, and those requiring the dummy auxiliary *(do).* From a semantic point of view none of these is of interest. This is in no way to suggest that they should not be of concern to language teachers who will, quite rightly, be concerned about the classroom. These points are not, however, difficult to understand, and it has been understanding which is the focus of this book.

20. Simple terminology for the English verb

The traditional terminology used to describe English verb forms is based on the terminology used to describe Latin. The Latin verb was highly inflected (it had 96 forms!) but the English verb is hardly inflected at all. Even irregular English verbs have only five forms:

take   takes   taking   took   taken

Modern language teachers are sometimes familiar with the terminology used to describe, for example, French or Spanish verbs. These two are much more highly inflected than English and possess more tense forms.

This book suggests a new, simpler terminology to describe the English verb forms. The terminology should fulfil two criteria:

Does the term accurately describe how the form is used?

Will the term, if not actually helping the student to understand, at least avoid potential confusion in the student's mind?

The old Latin terminology fails on both counts. The form normally called the present simple, for example, is frequently used for actions or events which are not associated with Present Time. In the same way the defining characteristic of those forms usually called past simple is *not* their association with Past Time. A term like 'present perfect' does not confuse in the same way, but that name in no way reflects the use of the form.

The simple terminology suggested in this book is sufficient to describe *all* common English verb forms. It has two clear advantages over the present terminology — the names are not misleading and reflect the use of the form and, because they are in themselves simple, they avoid students having to learn unnecessarily complicated meta-language.

The terms which are suggested in this book are listed below, together with examples of their use and the most frequently-used traditional terminology.

I hope teachers will, where possible, adopt this simplified terminology for their own classes. The reasons for each suggested term are given in the appropriate chapter.

Simple terminology for the English verb

Suggested terminology	Traditional terminology	Example
1. **The basic form** (The first form) **(b)**	Infinitive **(a)** Present simple Imperative	*take* I *speak* very poor Spanish *Sit* Down!
2. **The remote form** (The second form)	Past Simple	He *went* yesterday. He *said* he *understood.* I'd ask him if I *saw* him.
3. **The Compound form** **(c)** (The third form)	Past participle	He had *taken* the train. He was *brought* from London by car.
4. **Retrospective forms** Present retrospective **(d)** Past retrospective	Perfect forms Present perfect Past perfect	*(have)* + *3rd form* I've just seen him. I'd already *heard.*
5. **Prospective forms** Present prospective Past prospective	(No name)	It's *going to rain.* I *was going to tell* you anyway.
6. **Durative forms** (Limited duration)**(e)** Present durative Past durative	Continuous/progressive Present continuous/ progressive Past continuous/ progressive	*(be)* + *...ing* I'm *waiting for* Ann. I *was hoping* you'd ring.
7. **Passive**	Passive	It *was written* by Shake- speare.
8. **Auxiliary (f)**	Auxiliary verb	*Have, be, can, will* etc.
9. **The dummy auxiliary**	(No name)	*(do)* See Chapter 7.
10. **Question tag**	Question tag see Chapter 19	There's one in King Street, *isn't there?*
Invitation tag	Question tag	That was very enjoy- able *wasn't it.*

Notes

a. Many textbooks currently use the term 'infinitive' for items such as *to go, to walk.* The term should more properly be applied to *go, walk.* The form with *to* is then referred to as either 'the *to* infinitive' or 'the infinitive with *to*'. The point is of only academic interest for those adopting the terminology suggested in this chapter.

b. The term *first form, second form, third form* are useful when referring to the forms learned by students for irregular verbs as *go - went- gone, take - took- taken,* etc.

c. The term 'past participle' can be confusing as the form is used to make the *present* perfect and all forms of the passive. Most uses of the form, however, are with an auxiliary. For this reason it can be useful to refer to it as the compound form although, as the form only needs to be referred to in the case of irregular verbs, *the third form* is the term preferred in this book.

d. This may be combined with other forms, so that terms such as *past retrospective durative* will also be appropriate *(I had been expecting that).*

e. While the term *limited duration form* is the most accurately descriptive (see Chapter 12), it is also rather cumbersome. For this reason the term *durative form* is adopted. Some people may prefer *time-restricted* form which also conveys the essential characteristics of *(be)+. . .ing* forms.

For those who wish to avoid all terminology, these forms can,of course, be referred to simply as *(be) +. . .ing* forms.

f. It is better for students to learn auxiliaries as grammatical items which behave in certain ways rather than see them as 'defective verbs'. For this reason it is better to refer to them only as auxiliaries, rather then 'auxiliary verbs'.

This is somewhat more important in the case of the modal auxiliaries (see Chapter 13) where the term "modal auxiliary verb" easily leads to the idea that, for example, *could* is "the past tense" of *can*. This small change in terminology will not solve such problems, but may help to avoid some of them.

Other confusing terms

Although strictly outside the scope of this book, other careless terminology is used in modern language teaching:

i) Too often books and teachers are careless about the distinction between *singular/plural* and *countable/uncountable.* The verb in *The boy was waiting* is singular because the subject is singular — the verb in *Cheese is good for you* is singular because the subject is *uncountable,* **not** because it is singular. Although students have difficulty when, for example, a word is plural in their own language and uncountable in English, I have yet to find students who find it difficult to understand the difference — the difficulties seem to arise in *applying* the difference, particularly spontaneously.

If the distinction between *singular/plural* is confused with the (more fundamental) distinction *countable/uncountable,* confusion does arise with examples like:

The government is determined that. . .
The government were unable to agree on the issue.

ii) In one area a return to Latinate terminology could help. Latin nouns belonged to "the first declension" or "the second declension" while French nouns were "masculine" or "feminine". These latter terms are misleading. Why not describe nouns in French or German as simply Group 1, Group 2, etc. Instead of using terms which must seem at the very least, strange to students?

iii) The terminology which is appropriate for the English verb will not be suitable to describe, for example, the forms of the French, German or

Spanish verbs. Teachers of these languages should ask themselves whether the current terminology fulfils two basic criteria:

Does the term accurately describe the structure in question?

Does it avoid confusing the students, or unnecessarily burdening their memories?

Such terms as *aorist* and *imperfect* fail on both counts. Perhaps one of the difficulties of modern language teaching is the use of such undescriptive, confusing and unnecessarily obscure terminology. Even if teachers cannot immediately introduce more accurately descriptive terms, they could introduce 'neutral' descriptions such as using *(be) + . . .ing forms* to describe a structure of the English verb.

21. Some implications for the classroom

This book has predominantly been about English, rather than the teaching of English. At the same time I believe some of its suggestions have important implications for the classroom. These affect both *what* is studied and *how* it is studied.

The basic contention of the book is that almost all English verb forms are generated by a combination of a small number of structural features, each of which has clearly defined and identifiable primary semantic characteristics. The search for, and discussion of these, has formed the bulk of this book. At the same time, attention has been drawn to the fact that many traditional explanations are untrue, based on fundamentally misguided assumptions, and likely to confuse rather than help. The first and most obvious conclusion for the classroom is that teachers must stop presenting the so-called "simplified" explanations, which are the source of so much confusion. The following is taken from a book for teachers:

> The above is, of course, not all-embracing and does not pretend to be — but it does give a firm basis for question and answer exercises, and will not lead pupils into error.
> . . . as this exception can be very confusing to pupils, it is suggested that the teacher should only practise this in advanced classes and not mention this possibility unless an example of it happens to arise from a text or during conversation.

This must be misguided. While it would be over-ambitious to present a huge random collection of examples to students in the early stages of learning, it must be equally foolish to "hide" examples. This mistake is based on an important assumption which I believe to be wholly false. It is that an important part of language teaching consists of the teacher *explaining* "grammar". Many of the simplified but false "explanations" discussed in this book are based on the idea that the teacher should explain, and that unless the explanations are simplified "the students won't understand". Central to this argument is the fact that it is good for the students to understand these "explanations". Many teachers see this assumption as a self-evident fact. I believe it is neither self-evident nor even true!

At the end of most of the central chapters of this book there is a brief summary. In most cases, in a few lines the primary semantic characteristics of an important feature of the English verb are described. The content of some 200 pages can be reduced to a few brief summaries. Most readers will, I'm sure however, be willing to agree that the summaries alone would be useless. Ideas such as the non-temporality of the "present simple" and "past simple" or the judgmental quality of the modal auxiliary, can be defined in a few words, but can only be understood through *exploring* examples, description of the examples, and the relationship between the descriptions and the examples. "Understanding" is not a matter of knowing the conclusions outlined in a summary, but is the *process* of guessing, checking, formulating a description, finding fault with it, re-guessing, and slowly working towards a more explicit understanding of what is initially only implicit and intuitive.

There can be no point in explaining to students, if they do not understand the explanation, or if it is of no use to them. Many of the traditional grammar explanations are untrue, relate only to a limited range of examples, and are a source of potential confusion. More surprisingly perhaps, it seems to me from considering more general and more accurate explanations that they are of very limited use in the classroom. They are certainly not "the answer" to more efficient language teaching. In general, I believe language teaching should be much more orientated towards teaching students skills, and towards working with larger, less-controlled pieces of language. However, it seems clear that there are times when some students are helped by introspecting about the language. Part, and probably a smaller part than many teachers believe, of a balanced language teaching programme, should provide students with this opportunity. This will not be achieved by conventional grammar practices.

An essential characteristic of practices which permit this linguistic introspection, will be that they are centred upon student activity rather than the teacher talking. A second characteristic will be that the material which is being explored has been selected to permit the discovery of patterns, or semantic characteristics.

As Christopher Candlin has pointed out, the formation of hypotheses, and the testing of these against data is a natural and important part of the teaching of most subjects, *except* languages, in schools. An attitude which encourages the forming of hypotheses, the examination of language data, and the re-formation of the hypotheses — all work done by the students co-operatively under the guidance but not dominance of the teacher — are characteristics of a genuinely communicative approach to language teaching.

Before any practice is to be successful, however, teachers must ensure that their students know, and more importantly feel, certain basic principles.

Some principles for the classroom

I would suggest that all foreign language courses should begin by drawing to students' attention the fact that they must *never* expect the foreign language to be like their own. Teachers should not just *tell* students this, but discuss it, heightening their awareness both of usage in their own language, and of the difference of the foreign language. There are many examples which are sufficiently simple for even young students: the English contrast between *a/an* and the strong form *one;* for many European students English *you* contrasts with a choice of two or even three forms in their own language; the fact that English has verb forms which contain *(have)* as an auxiliary does not suggest that other languages "ought to" have a corresponding form, or that if another language has a form which contains the equivalent verb the meanings of the two forms are related in any way. I believe teachers should emphasise these differences by choosing clear examples where an *apparent* similarity is, in fact, a difference. Every English student of French, for example, would like *j'ai donné* to mean *I have given*, rather than *I gave*. Students should positively be encouraged to *expect* the foreign language to be different and, as far as possible, to explore the foreign language within itself, rather than through the expectations they bring from their own.

The important distinction between grammar as fact and grammar as choice was discussed in Chapter 5. It is important for all students to acquire an understanding of this distinction, without perhaps using those terms. At first it is of little importance, but as students progress, questions of the type *Is . . . also possible? Why?* frequently arise. In some cases the difference can be explained; in others the difference is the speaker's view or attitude. Unless students have understood that this is a *possible* way of explaining such difference, teachers who use it, however validly, will seem to be "explaining away", not explaining. At the lowest levels students can be asked how, in their own language, they would greet a school friend, their grandmother, an elderly neighbour, and their headmaster. They are most unlikely to produce the same expression for all four occasions. Teachers can then discuss why they have chosen different expressions for the different occasions — what factors influenced them; what other expressions fulfilling the same function can they list?

On a more complex level teachers can prepare in advance expressions in the students' own native language which reflect the difference in English between:

Are you going?
Aren't you going?
You are going, aren't you?

Students are then asked the difference between the sentences in their own language. With even more advanced students they may be asked to produce English translations which reflect the different expectations of the speaker exhibited in the examples in their own language.

The distinction between grammar as fact, and grammar as choice is much more than a theoretical distinction. It has important practical consequences for the kind of work which teachers can do to broaden the intellectual horizons of, and encourage understanding in, "ordinary" school students. It can make students more aware of their own language, their own use of it and the way language in general is used around them.

Sorting practices

There is no point in asking students to manipulate structures which they have not correctly perceived. There is no reason why a teacher should draw students' attention to a pattern which they can discover for themselves. All learning theory suggests that those things which we discover for ourselves are more firmly fixed in our minds than those which we are "told". This suggests that one activity appropriate to the classroom is to mimic the process that the descriptive grammarian has gone through. It is through sorting that we find the patterns of the language. If students sort correctly, there is more chance of them remembering than if they had been told. If students sort incorrectly, the misunderstanding will be clear and can be dealt with before building on an insecure foundation.

On the simplest level it is not necessary to *tell* students the difference between, for example, questions with *do* and those with *does;* a sorting practice is more appropriate. Students are presented with a group of examples and asked to divide the examples into groups, usually, as in this case, two. Here is a set appropriate to the *do/does* distinction:

1. Does he speak German?	6. Do you take milk?
2. Does he know her?	7. Do you like tennis?
3. Do they know her?	8. Does he play tennis?
4. Does she play tennis?	9. Do you come from London?
5. Does he work?	10. Do they have a car?

The examples may be chosen to reveal a rule, or a partial rule. In this case, the contrast may be introduced between *Do you* and *Does he/she* or the more general, complete, contrast *Do I/we/you/they/* v. *Does he/she/it.* The point is a simple one — rather than *presenting* and *telling* the students the distinction, they are allowed to discover it for themselves. Techniques of this kind are common in many school subjects, particularly in science and mathematics. They could be introduced equally successfully into language teaching.

A truly communicative methodology naturally suggests a classroom where students work together with language, examining carefully-chosen input materials. The emphasis moves from learning to use, to *learning through using.*

Here are some examples of sorting practices of varying levels of difficulty. In most cases the practices can be made slightly more difficult by adding more, and slightly more varied, examples. These practices are only examples of the kind of practice which can usefully be introduced.

Practice 1
Sort these examples into two groups.

1. He's done it.	5. He's taken it.
2. It's raining.	6. Where's he going?
3. Who's that?	7. What's the matter?
4. It's not mine.	8. Who's taking it?

Practice 2
Sort these examples into two groups — those where *'d* represents *had* and those where it does not.

1. I'd rather not, if you don't mind.	5. What'd they done about it.
2. I'd be delighted.	6. He'd be surprised.
3. She'd already got one.	7. How long'd you been waiting.
4. He'd done it.	8. Who'd've thought that it was him.

Practice 3
Divide these sentences into two groups. What's the difference between them.

1. The dog stole it!	6. They haven't heard yet.
2. Someone's coming up the stairs.	7. You can leave the car here.
3. The telephone was ringing.	8. He can play the violin very well
4. I wrote the number down.	9. He plays the piano too.
5. I feel sick.	10. It's started to rain.

(Those with/without an auxiliary)

Practice 4

Divide these into two groups. What is the difference between them?

1. I've asked twice already.
2. I have asked twice already.
3. That would be nice.
4. I'm sure he'd be pleased with that.
5. They are trying to help!
6. They're looking for it at the moment.

Now sort these examples into the same two groups:

7. I expected to hear before now.
8. He told me it was easy to find.
9. You did promise to ring me.
10. He will be there on Saturday.

(Stressed/unstressed auxiliary)

Why is it difficult to know which group these examples belong to?

11. He was trying to help you.
12. He can drive.

(There is no conventional way of writing the *can/was* weak forms)

Practice 5

Sort these into two groups. What is the difference between them?

1. It's going to rain.
2. What are we going to do about it?
3. Are you going to tell anybody?
4. I'm going to the cinema this evening.
5. Where are you going?
6. We're going to Ibiza this summer.
7. Are you going to go to the match on Saturday?
8. Is anyone going with you?

(Full verb *(go)* v auxiliary *(be) going to.*)

Practice 6

Sort these examples into two groups. Say what the general difference of meaning is between the two groups.

1. It's raining again.
2. I'm staying in a hotel in George Street.
3. I'm not feeling very well.
4. I come from Birmingham.
5. He drives an old Ford Escort.
6. I'm waiting for a phone call.
7. I'm afraid she's not feeling well.
8. It rains quite a lot in the North.
9. It takes about an hour and a half.
10. Are you taking your umbrella?

("present simple"/"present continuous"; the semantics of the *(be)* + . . .*ing* forms)

Practice 7

Sort these examples into two groups. What is the difference of *meaning* between the two groups?

1. It was made in Portugal.
2. She's wearing a dark blue dress.
3. She wore a dark blue dress.
4. The general ordered them to attack.
5. It was opened by the Queen.
6. It was built in 1937.
7. They were ordered to attack.
8. We were taken to the airport by taxi.

Here is a more difficult set of sentences with the same basic distinction.

1. They've been waiting for you for ages.
2. Somebody's been trying to get in touch with you.
3. That was being built when I was here last year.
4. We're having a new carpet fitted.
5. They're taking their time!
6. I'll be writing to you shortly.
7. You'll be hearing from me shortly.
8. I think the road must be being repaired at the moment.

This set is difficult. It can be made more so, and an interesting unusual use may be introduced, by asking students to sort the examples just given together with the two which follow into *three* groups:

9. We've just had the sitting room decorated.
10. I've just had my hair done.

In the case of the three-way sort, examples 9 and 10 should be mixed with the other examples rather than put as the last two as here.

These sets both investigate the form *and meaning* of the passive. They provide a basis for discussion and exploration at an advanced level.

Practice 8

Sort these sentences into two groups. What is the basic *structural* difference between them? Can you explain why the two groups are different in *meaning?*

1. Oh dear, I'm going to sneeze.
2. Philip's coming to see us on Saturday.
3. I'm going to see my grandmother at the weekend.
4. I'm taking my exam in June.
5. He's going to be a ballet dancer.
6. I'm afraid it's going to rain again.
7. The children are starting school again next week.
8. Don't forget we're having dinner early this evening.

Practice 9

Sort these sentences into two groups. What is the difference of meaning between the two groups?

1. You mustn't take life so seriously.
2. You needn't wait for me if I'm not there at 1 o'clock.
3. You mustn't be surprised if he shouts, he's like that.
4. You mustn't forget to send me a postcard.
5. You needn't take your umbrella, it's clearing up.
6. You needn't worry, it'll be all right.
7. You mustn't worry, it'll be all right.
8. You mustn't get the 8 o'clock train — it doesn't stop at Padgate.

Practice 10

Sort these sentences into two groups. Can you see any general difference of meaning between the two groups?

1. You have to leave your camera at the cloakroom.
2. You'll have to get there early.
3. I'm afraid you'll have to wait until I've washed my hands.
4. You have to press that little red button.
5. It has to be cooked for 40 minutes.
6. I'll have to ring him when I get home this evening.
7. I'm afraid I have to wear spectacles nowadays.
8. If you've forgotten your own, you'll have to borrow one.

Practice 11

Sort these examples into *three* groups. What are the differences between the groups?

1. I used to live in York.
2. I'm not used to driving in this heavy traffic.
3. I'll never get used to this new system.
4. People used to be more polite.
5. It takes a long time for people to get used to new ideas.
6. My leg's still pretty bad, but I'm getting used to it now.
7. Have you got used to living on the tenth floor yet?
8. I'm not really used to getting up so early in the morning.
9. I used to drink a lot more tea than I do nowadays.
10 We didn't use to drink much coffee.

The next practices are slightly different; they still ask students to sort examples but, rather than simply sorting into groups, they have to examine characteristics of particular examples.

Practice 12

Sort these examples into two groups — those where the event referred to is *before* the moment of speaking, and those where the event referred to is *after* the moment of speaking. Do all the examples belong in one category, or are there some in each?

1. I was going to see her tomorrow.
2. We were going to ask David to come with us next week.
3. I was going to see him, but he wasn't in the office yesterday.
4. We were going to catch the early train but I'm afraid we slept in.
5. Oh, hello, I'm glad you've called, I was just going to ring you.
6. Were you going to take your car or would you like to come with me?
7. If you hadn't got some money, I was going to go to the bank.
8. Now, what was I going to say . . . ah yes, . . .

The fact that the examples of this practice can be sorted into two categories — some before Now and some after Now, means that this is *not* a defining characteristic of *was/were going to*. In this case the practice makes clear that a boundary of meaning which the student may think exists does not in fact do so. This contrasts with most sorting practices which draw attention to a boundary of meaning.

Practice 13

Could always represents 'remoteness'. Divide these examples into different groups, each showing a different kind of remoteness. Try to label the different groups appropriately.

1. Could you pass the salt please.
2. I don't know what we could do about it.
3. I couldn't find it anywhere.
4. I couldn't do it even if I tried.
5. Could we say half past ten tomorrow morning?
6. I'd be grateful if you could.
7. Who else could we ask?
8. Could I get you another cup of tea?
9. How could I have known?
10. My father could tell exactly where anybody came from by their accent.

This practice, while emphasising the underlying unity of meaning of *could* draws attention to what in traditional grammatical terms are "different uses" of the form.

I must emphasise that I am not suggesting these practices as an alternative to conventional, productive practices. If these are an alternative to anything, it is to conventional *presentation,* where the teacher isolates a particular language feature and talks about it. These practices are more involving and are themselves useful activities, contributing to a student's general education. Those given above are mostly intermediate or advanced but similar practices which are much simpler, introducing distinctions such as *was/were* or *is/was* can be used. They may be based either on examples specially written or on carefully chosen texts. The emphasis is on encouraging student observation and involvement, and encouraging students to hypothesise, test their hypothesis, re-formulate etc. In place of blind 'learning', the emphasis is moved to the process of exploration which leads to genuine understanding.

Diagrams

Reference books, textbooks, and teachers frequently try to make the significance of particular verb forms clearer for students by the use of diagrams. Such diagrams are analogies, and like all analogies are dangerous. Providing we are aware of the limitations — and in two cases the limitations are very severe — diagrams can be a source of help. First, we must establish one point on which diagrams are certain to cause confusion rather than help.

We have discussed extensively in this book that the two pure tense forms — the "present simple" and the "past simple" — do not express fundamentally temporal concepts. In each case these forms are appropriate if the speaker conceptualises the action as a pure fact, immediate or remote, but without reference to a temporal frame. Although an event such as *I lived there for 30 years* happened in time, that sentence, despite the adverbial, is not, essentially a temporal reference. The consequence of this is that **any** attempt to draw it "in time" will be a **mis**-representation.

The same problem occurs in a slightly different form with the "present simple". This form is appropriate if the speaker has an immediate, and undivided view of the event. It is appropriate for forms which may be identified with the moment of speaking: *I pronounce you man and wife.* It is also appropriate for events which are undivided in their generality: *Water boils at 100° C.* With a temporal framework, these two types of event are quite distinct — one is located at the point Now, while the other is co-equal with time, extending infinitely on either side of Now. They appear completely different from each other. This is because the verb form is used because of the nature of the speaker's conceptualisation of the events, not because of any temporal framework. Imposing the temporal framework *creates* an apparent difference.

The first warning, then, is that any diagram attempting a temporal interpretation of the two pure tense forms is likely to be a misrepresentation, and a source of confusion.

The second important preparatory point to any system of diagrams, is to emphasise that the drawings do not represent the real time occupied by an event. They are representations of the speaker's perception, what we called earlier psychological time. Unless students have grasped clearly the ideas of the importance of the speaker, and of grammar as choice, *any* diagram system is potentially confusing. To argue that this is unnecessarily complicated for language students is a fundamental misunderstanding. Nobody can explain individual sentences out of context in a satisfactory and coherent way. It is almost always possible to say whether a sentence is well-formed or not, but frequently the significance of the individual choices made by the speaker may only be guessed at. This importance of the speaker and the corresponding importance of psychological time, cannot be over-estimated.

The fact that any diagram represents psychological time not real time is probably the greatest source of difficulty in introducing such diagrams into the classroom.

Providing the two warnings just discussed are borne in mind, time-line sketches of verb phrases can be of assistance to students. They need first to be introduced to the idea of the time line, and to the "most interesting" point on it, the point Now. It is essential that they understand that this is not "now", but means "the moment of speaking". The time-line extends endlessly in both directions:

NOW

In Chapter 6 the reader was invited to consider different possible distinctions. In fact, we may conceptualise and draw the following:

A point   **A limited period**

Periods "unlimited in both directions" are co-equal with time, or, alternatively exist "outside time". Such events are always expressed with a "present simple" verb form: *Like poles of a magnet repel each other.*

The most useful idea suggested by these diagrams is that all *(be)* + . . .*ing* forms are represented by the same **kind** of drawing. The primary semantic characteristic of *(be)* + . . .*ing* forms is that they represent limited periods. Such events are bi-punctual. They exist between *two* points and the speaker's interest is concentrated upon the *period* between the two points.

It was raining.   **It's raining.**

Any event which does not contain a *(be)* + . . .*ing* form, is not bi-punctual. It is either conceptualised as a single point, or one or more of the "end points" is missing:

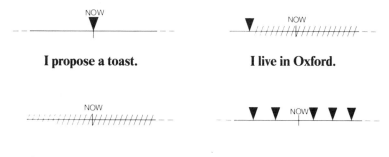

I propose a toast.   **I live in Oxford.**

Wood floats on water.   **I play tennis most weekends.**

The last example illustrates a feature which, at first sight, we might not have expected. In addition to points and periods we may also conceptualise *sequences*. Logically, these could be seen as significant, and be represented by a different verb form. In English, this is not so. Unlimited periods and unlimited sequences are represented by a simple verb form; limited periods and limited sequences by *(be)* + . . .*ing* forms.

It's raining.   **I'm taking the car every day this week.**

Diagrammatic representations of durative forms seem genuinely to help many students understand their significance. Readers are warned, however, of examples such as *I lived in Cambridge for 4 years*. This is extended in real time, and most students would argue it must be extended even in psychological time because of the time adverbial. In fact, we have already observed, the simple tense forms are not essentially based on temporal considerations. It is the nature of the factuality, immediate or remote, which is important. If a diagrammatic representation is to be used, it is only possible providing the convention is adopted that the speaker's total, undivided view of events expressed in the "past simple", is represented diagrammatically as a *point* in time — a dot on the time line. If the convention is adopted, the following diagrams are appropriate:

I lived in Cambridge for 4 years.   I was living in Cambridge for 4 years.

Diagrams are an analogy. The analogy breaks down if this convention is not adopted. Readers must judge for themselves whether the advantages of diagrams representing the durative forms, outweigh the potential disadvantage of introducing a convention. It is debatable whether the idea of a point representing the speaker's undivided view of the past event is helpful or otherwise.

In the main body of the book we have shown that "present" tenses do not always refer to Present Time etc. At the same time, in the context of a traditional syllabus, it is difficult to imagine teachers abandoning the strongly time-based system of teaching verb forms. It is, therefore, helpful to consider uses of the verb form which appear to have time reference of the kind traditionally imagined. A simple diagram may be built up, step by step, which illustrates some important feature of verbs with temporal reference.

The speaker may regard things as immediately present and, from a point of view at Now, may look *at* an event, *back* on an event or *forward* to an event. These views are expressed respectively by the use of the simple form, the retrospective form, and the prospective form. They may be illustrated diagrammatically thus:

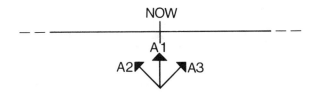

A1   *I swear it wasn't me*
A2   *I've seen him already.*
A3   *I'm going to see him tomorrow.*

The same kind of division — looking *at, back,* or *forward* is possible with remote forms, expressing the fact that the speaker views things from a point remote in time.

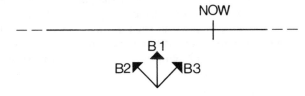

B1   *I saw him yesterday.*
B2   *I'd seen him before.*
B3   *I was going to see him in the afternoon.*

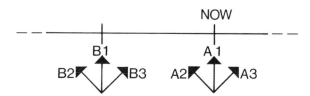

We have discussed at length that it is not possible to identify *will ('ll)* with Future Time. It is, however, common for this to have Future Time reference. If we confine our attention to *will ('ll)* forms with Future Time reference a similar three part diagram is possible for Future Time:

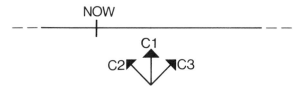

C1 *I'll see him tomorrow.*
C2 *I'll have seen him before Saturday.*
C3 *I'll be going to see him when I get to London.*

If we confine ourselves to *will ('ll)* with Future Time reference the full drawing of verb forms with temporal reference may be made:

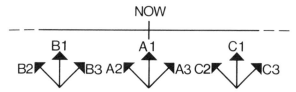

The (2) forms, expressing retrospection, are characterised by *(have) + third form;* and the (3) forms, expressing prospection, are characterised by *(be) going to.*

It is important to recognise that this diagram does not represent *all* uses of the forms in question, but is restricted to those which have specific time reference (as opposed, for example, to psychological or logical reference).

The above diagram does, however, represent a useful presentation for teaching purposes. It shows that there is a consistency of usage; all retrospective forms, which are easily seen on the diagram to be retrospective, are characterised by *(have) + third form,* etc. It expresses concisely and visually what was traditionally expressed in such terminology as "the future in the past" *(He was going to ask me)*. Within limitations, this diagram does depict many English verb forms with temporal reference. To the forms described above (A1 - C3) must be added:

(i)   the formation of questions,
(ii) the formation of negatives,
(iii) the formation of the passive,
(iv) the durative forms, characterised by *(be) +...ing.*

The "present simple" represented on this diagram is a relatively infrequent use, i.e. the use which is associated with actions located precisely at the moment of speaking, the point Now. Uses of this form with general time reference *(Wood floats on water)* in which the representation of the action would be coincident with the time line itself, cannot usefully be depicted on the diagram. This does not undermine the essential identity of all uses of the basic form; it merely indicates that diagrammatic representations are analogies, covering only a restricted range of uses. While not useful as an initial teaching presentation, I have found it provides many students who are dissatisfied with "rules and exceptions" explanations, with an explanation which they find satisfying, reassuring and helpful.

Directional diagrams

It is also possible to represent diagrammatically the retrospective and prospective forms. Each of these is bi-punctual and *directional;* in the one case the speaker looks *back* and in the other *forward*. They are, therefore, appropriately represented by an arrow linking the two points and pointing in the appropriate direction:

I've met him before.   **I'm going to see him tomorrow.**

It will be noted that, like durative forms, these are bi-punctual and, at first sight, the first diagram above appears to depict a durative form; this is not the case. The present retrospective looks back from the point Now to a *point* in the past so that the following diagram is appropriate:

I've met him before.

The speaker's interest is concentrated upon an event conceptualised at the moment of speaking as a single, undivided unit in the past. It is, of course, possible for the speaker's interest at the moment of speaking to be concentrated on a *period* in the past — then, as we would expect, a durative form is appropriate and may be represented diagrammatically thus:

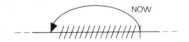

I've been looking everywhere for you.

The distinction between *I've met him before* and *I've been looking everywhere for you* is the speaker's interest in an undivided event in the past, or a period in the past; the two diagrams draw attention to this difference.

Diagrams of verb forms will certainly not solve all our problems. It is, for example, impossible to devise diagrams to depict the choice of verb form with reference to Future Time. The advantage of diagrams is that many students who find verbal explanations difficult to follow will benefit from this technique. It is particularly useful in clarifying durative forms, but also helpful in dealing with retrospective and prospective forms. Within limits, it is a helpful way of making accessible to students some of the essential characteristics of the structure and meaning of the English verb.

There is no reason why students need to adopt the particular symbols described above. At first students need be given no more guidance than for the teacher to suggest **a** method for depicting points and a method for depicting periods. As with sorting problems, teachers must not be in too much of a hurry. Wrong drawings, preferably corrected by other students, lead towards an understanding of the form which is more profound than nodding politely at the teacher's verbal explanation.

Teachers may care to try the following list of sentences, inviting their classes to depict these on the time-line:

1. It's raining.
2. It rains every summer.
3. It takes 45 minutes by train.
4. The phone is ringing.
5. I see what you mean.
6. They cost about £6 each.
7. They usually show a good film on Saturday evenings.
8. I'm thinking about it.
9. I think he's French.
10. I feel sick.
11. I live in London.
12. I'm living in Castle Road.

If the students can depict these on the time-line, and recognise that the characteristic of all *(be)* + . . .*ing* forms is that they exist between "two crosses", they will be well on the way to understanding the significance of durative forms.

Theoreticians are agreed that language learning is a cyclical process — students will constantly return to the same grammatical forms developing increasing understanding of those forms and of their varied contextual uses. Frequently language teachers pay only lip-service to this idea. It is not a disaster if students do not "understand the present continuous" the first time it is presented to them. Understanding of the concept is to be built up over a period using examples, verbal explanation, and sorting practices and diagrams of the kind discussed in this chapter. It is important to remember that languages are different and that the distinctions of English are new and unusual ideas to the speakers of another language. It would be extremely surprising if they were understood and mastered in a single lesson; patience is required.

Finally, it needs to be repeated that, while there is every point in providing students with particular help for a certain exercise, or even an individual example *(Notice the 'not', Is he doing it at the moment?)*, these hints must not be confused with accurately-stated grammar rules. Teachers who remember the distinction and ensure that their students are aware of it, will avoid much wasted class time and increase their students' confidence in their ability to learn the language. The fact that practical difficulties make genuine understanding difficult to achieve is no justification for abandoning it as an important and realistic objective in the whole learning process.

22. Immediate improvements

I hope many teachers in training will understand the explanations provided in this book, see their usefulness, and from the beginning of their teaching careers incorporate the ideas into their teaching. On an entirely practical level, I should like to end by suggesting some specific practical changes which *any* language teacher could introduce immediately. Each suggestion is simple, easy to carry out, and will in some small way help. Some emphasise things which teachers should *not* do; some introduce new activities.

1. Avoid unnecessary terminology.

Stop using any terms which students do not understand, and, if possible, use simpler names. Remember no terminology is intended to make the teacher sound impressive, it is supposed to help students.

2. Avoid constant reference to the student's native language.

The important grammatical distinctions of English are internal to English. The basic form contrasts with the remote, or with the present durative. It is these distinctions students have to understand. It is unnecessarily confusing if teachers are constantly contrasting how something is said in English with how it is said in the student's native language.

3. Avoid "sometimes" rules.

All statements of the kind "*must* is sometimes stronger than *have to*", are meaningless. Information is no help unless the distinction between the occasions when the statement is true and those when it is not true is clear. "Explanations" which include *sometimes,* are not explanations at all.

4. Avoid giving a rule then finding examples to fit it.

The language comes first, the descriptions or rules later. It is often easy to invent an example which fits a "rule" which you have already invented. It is also short-sighted — if the "rule" is not true, the difficulties and confusion which arise when students meet examples which do not fit will be of your own making.

5. Avoid isolated examples.

Language acquires its full communicative meaning only in context. Sometimes it may be necessary for students to study a verb *form.* For this, a single sentence may be helpful. A single sentence in isolation will almost never help in the study of *meaning*. For this, it will be necessary to study examples in context, groups of examples, or contrasting examples.

6. Avoid creating confusion.

If a distinction is not fully clear to you, there is no point in presenting it to students. If they ask questions, you must be able to answer them clearly and confidently. This is almost impossible with such old chestnuts as the *should/ would* distinction. The implication is that such contrasts should not be presented.

7. Avoid artificial "simplification".

There is no point at all in pretending that *will/shall* is *"the* future". If it solves a problem in Unit 12 of your coursebook, it only makes a bigger problem in Unit 15. Of course it is necessary for teachers sometimes to simplify but, if they do this, they should always make it clear to students that what they are studying is not generally true, and is only a temporary helpful hint.

8. Avoid emphasising difficulty.

Teachers can help students by being realistic about the simplicity or difficulty of a task. Some things are more difficult than others, and they become slightly less frightening if you know you are not going to understand immediately. At the same time, teachers can sometimes make language learning seem impossible with remarks like *English is a very difficult language, English is full of exceptions,* or *English is very illogical.* Such remarks are both untrue and unhelpful.

9. Avoid statements you know are untrue.

It is sometimes impossible to tell students the whole truth. Many of the explanations in this book are quite unsuitable for presentation in the school classroom. At the same time, this is not a justification for presenting nonsense simplifications which the teacher knows will lead to a long string of exceptions later. All *classroom* explanation is a compromise between accuracy and understandability. Too often — as with the famous "explanation" of *some/any* — teachers go much too far in one direction.

10. Avoid confusing "explaining" and "understanding".

All too often teachers explain to save time. It is very doubtful how much time is saved. First, it is necessary that the teacher's explanation is accurate. Secondly, and much more importantly, it does not follow that because the teacher has explained clearly, the students have understood. If they have not understood, no time has been saved at all. Instead, a problem has been stored up for later, students have been confused or intimidated, and the whole process of language learning made more difficult.

11. Explain the difference between a Rule and a Hint.

This book has been an exploration of general and rather abstract grammar rules. Many can clearly not be taken straight into the classroom. At the same time students sometimes need a hint to help them with a particular example or exercise. There is no harm in such hints, providing both the students and the teacher are fully aware that they are particular suggestions, tied to particular examples. Teachers need to explain the difference between a general rule and a classroom hint early in the students' course, and to remind them of it at appropriate times during the course.

12. Emphasise meaning.

Remember that language is not about forms, but about meaning. There is no point in students knowing the forms, if they do not understand and cannot use the language to convey meaning. In many ways dissecting the language in order to teach it is counter-productive. The student who does not see the point of exercises which practise only the forms of language (*Put the following sentences in the passive*) is right. Language is not a set of formal rules to be operated like a very complicated game. It is used because somebody wants to say something. Language teaching which does not place meaning at the centre, is not *language* teaching at all.

13. Be prepared to change.

If you meet an example which does not fit a "rule" which you learned years ago, there is no point in discarding the example — it is the "rule" which has to go!

Because you have always explained a particular grammatical point in a certain way, it does not mean you have to explain it the same way next time. Indeed, it doesn't even mean that you have to *explain* it at all!

14. Remember the importance of stress and intonation.

Avoid teaching "the short form" as a synonym for "the spoken form". Students need to understand the important contribution made to meaning by stress and intonation. They need to know both the stressed and unstressed forms, and the fact that there is a difference of meaning between them.

15. Explain both elements of significance in durative forms.

Durative forms are used when the speaker refers to a limited period. Both parts of the explanation are important — it is a *period,* and it is *limited.* Many traditional classroom explanations ignore the importance of one or other of these elements.

16. Emphasise regularity where it will help.

Teachers often place too much emphasis on irregularity and contrast. Instead of talking about 'the present continuous used as the future' as if it were completely different from the 'ordinary' present continuous, encourage students to see what the two have in common.

Much of this book has been devoted to the search for the primary semantic characteristics of particular forms. Similarity of meaning has been of central importance. So it should be in the classroom. English is a coherent, understandable system. Too often, through over-emphasis on irregularity, students are given the impression that the task they are undertaking in learning a language is impossible.

17. Contrast English with English.

However the textbook presents language items, it is essential that from time to time students study the *contrast* between language forms e.g. present simple/ continuous, present perfect/past simple, *can/may, must/have to, can/could* etc.

Presenting students with contrasting items, and inviting them to say why they think the items are different (*not* explaining the difference to them) is a small, but important, part of a well-balanced language teaching programme. Teachers will improve their language teaching immediately if, instead of constantly contrasting English with the student's native tongue, they change the emphasis to English/English contrasts.

18. Make language teaching part of a wider educational perspective.

Language teaching is about many things. Language itself is many things — at the moment communication is frequently emphasised. The central grammatical problems of language, however, are also a *system*. And, as we have seen in this book, a system that is coherent and comprehensible. One of the more general aims of language teaching, as part of general education, is to encourage students to see the world as analysable and understandable. A small part of language teaching can usefully be spent concentrating on the idea of language as system.

19. Take time.

Most of the explanations in this book can be phrased in a very few words. But like most explanations, however accurate and however succinct, used alone they are useless. The central grammatical problems of English, or any other language, may involve understanding ideas which may be completely new. This takes time, and can only be done effectively by combining example, explanation, guessing, etc. There is no short cut — and the teacher providing explanations is certainly no short cut, only a *small* part of the complex process of learning.

20. Stop explaining, start exploring.

Give students a chance to guess — and therefore a chance to show that they mis-understand. In the end, it is the degree of student involvement which is important. Exploring in pairs, in groups, and *with* the teacher is more exciting and more helpful than any explanation given *by* the teacher.

Postscript

I have attacked many traditional classroom explanations in this book. I can think of nothing more unsatisfactory than that teachers should now take the explanations offered in this book and present them to their students!

I believe it is essential for teachers to have a clear and deep understanding of the central structures of the language they are teaching. I do not, however, believe that explanation has anything other than a very small part to play in the normal school classroom. I beg the reader not to impose the rather abstract explanations of this book on their unsuspecting students.